FARM JOURNAL'S PICNIC & BARBECUE COOKBOOK

Farm Journal's
PICNIC & BARBECUE
Cookbook

By the Food Editors of Farm Journal

Edited by Patricia A. Ward
Farm Journal Food Editor

Farm Journal, Inc.
Philadelphia, Pennsylvania

Library of Congress Cataloging in Publication Data
Main entry under title:
Farm journal's picnic and barbecue cookbook
Includes index.
1. Picnicking. 2. Outdoor cookery. 3. Barbecue cookery.
I. Ward, Patricia A., 1943- . II. Farm journal (Philadel-
phia, Pa. :1956) III. Title: Picnic and barbecue cookbook.
TX823.F35   641.5'78   82-1518
ISBN: 0-89795-013-5

Book Design by Michael P. Durning
Color photographs by William Hazzard/
Hazzard Studios (facing pp. 38, 102 and 103);
and Mel Richman Studios (facing p. 39).

Contents

Introduction   *vii*

Let's Eat Outdoors!   1

Using These Recipes   1
Packing the Picnic Basket   1
Equipping the Outdoor Kitchen   5
Charcoal Cooking Know-How   7
Let It Rain!   8

Springtime Celebrations   9

Steak and Potatoes to Go   10
"Spring Forward" Brunch   12
Alfresco American-style   14
Pick-Me-Up Picnic   16
May Day Feast   18
Pizza Burger Barbecue   20
Low-Cal Cookout   22
Backyard Barbecue   24
Springtime Jubilee   26
Mother's Day Barbecue   28
Surprise Supper   30
Graduation Day Buffet   32
Chicken in a Basket   34
Mexican-style Supper   36
Impromptu Picnic   38
American Heritage Barbecue   40
Parade Party   42

Summer Reunions   45

Carefree Chicken Barbecue   46
Soup 'n' Sandwich Supper   48
A Moveable Feast   50
City-style Cookout   52
A Family Reunion   54
Pride of Iowa Barbecue   56
Father's Day Favorites   58
Supper on a Saber   60
Courtyard Cuisine   62

Hawaiian Luau   64
All-American Cookout   66
Fourth of July Picnic   68
Block Party Barbecue   70
Campers' Choice   72
Midsummer Night's Supper   74
Pick-Up-and-Go Picnic   76
Outdoor Kitchen Cookery   78
Happy Birthday Barbecue   80
Stop-and-Go Supper   82
Summertime Sandwichery   84
Community Cookout   86
Sombrero Supper   88
Little League Banquet   90
A Complete Meal on the Grill   92
Square Dance Supper   94
Lazy Day Barbecue   96
Prelude or Finale   98

Autumn Gatherings   101

Trail Blazer's Barbecue   102
Picnic in a Bag   104
Labor Day Recess   106
Dinner for a Dozen   108
Back-to-School Barbecue   110
Landlubber's Lunch   112
Anytime, Anyplace Picnic   114
Blue Sky Supper   116
Tailgate Picnic   118
Octoberfest   120
Chuckwagon Special   122
Pilgrims' Picnic   124
Potlatch Picnic   126
A Meal in the Field   128
Gourmet at the Grill   130
Post-Game Warm-up   132
Autumn Table   134

Index   137

COLOR PHOTOGRAPHS

FOLLOWING PAGE 38

Marinated Beef Kabobs

A Trio of Super Salads

A Moveable Feast

Simple Fruit Desserts

FOLLOWING PAGE 102

Impromptu Picnic

A Meal in the Field

Ginger-glazed Spareribs

Kansas-style Beef Tacos

Introduction

There's something about the outdoors that makes food taste better—a fresh breeze, an open space and a view of new surroundings have a way of turning a meal into something special. A picnic or barbecue is a practical way to enjoy a meal when you're on the go, and it's an ideal form of casual entertaining that family and friends of all ages can appreciate.

Picnicking is a way of life for many farm and ranch families, especially during the busy planting and harvesting seasons. Many farm women routinely take lunch to the field to help the crew save time; one young Pennsylvania woman rounds up her youngsters so they can all join Dad for a field picnic even on extra-busy days.

Barbecuing is increasingly popular among farm families, too, and thanks to convenient gas and electric grills, many farm women use their grills year 'round. To extend the barbecuing season, one Iowa farm woman moves her grill into an open garage when the weather turns cool. A Minnesota homemaker barbecues extra hamburgers and steaks during the summertime and freezes them; then, on a wintry day, she whisks the meat out of her freezer and into her microwave for a meal that tastes like it's right off the grill.

Last summer we asked the readers of *Farm Journal* Magazine for their favorite picnic and barbecue recipes, and we weren't surprised by their enthusiastic response—hundreds of favorite recipes served at family reunions, backyard barbecues and community cookouts. We moved our Test Kitchens outdoors to test these recipes; then we chose the best of the new, added a few of our own favorites, and organized them into menus for family suppers and casual company-style meals.

This book is the result of all our recipe testing and development: 250 recipes and more than 60 menus, plus basic information about packing, storing and grilling foods, to make all your outdoor meals a picnic.

—Patricia A. Ward

FARM JOURNAL'S PICNIC & BARBECUE COOKBOOK

Let's Eat Outdoors!

When the weather is just too nice to be inside, it's easy to move your meals outdoors. Just pack up the makings of a picnic or plan to cook over the coals. Here are all the basics you'll need to know, whether you're cooking for 50 or just for six.

Using These Recipes

Each sample menu in this cookbook lists several dishes for which recipes are given on either the same or the following page. For easy reference, these recipes are starred; occasionally, other dishes also are included as suggestions to help round out your menu.

IN ADVANCE: Nearly every recipe in this book can be prepared at least partially in advance, and these are keyed by a headline. Most advance preparation can be done the night before your picnic. Many of these recipes, such as gelatin salads and barbecue sauces, can be prepared entirely in advance, and all baked goods can be stored in your freezer so you'll always have them on hand for impromptu picnicking.

TO GRILL: Recipes to be cooked over the coals are so indicated, and recipes that must be cooked indoors, on the range top or in the oven, are identified by the headline TO COOK.

Some barbecue recipes were tested on covered grills and others on open grills, and this is indicated in each recipe. The cooking times given for barbecue recipes are approximate and should be used as guidelines; your own cooking time may vary because of the heat of your fire, the weather and the size of the portions. However, for best results, meats should be at room temperature before grilling.

Packing the Picnic Basket

You'll always be ready for an impromptu picnic if you store a few basics in a picnic basket, cooler or box:
- tablecloth
- plates, cups and flatware
- napkins
- salt, pepper, sugar
- can and bottle openers
- sharp knives
- serving spoons
- dish cloths and towels
- plastic wrap and aluminum foil
- plastic bag for cleanup

Enough for a crowd

Everyone seems to be a little hungrier than usual whenever food is served outdoors. If you're planning a family reunion or a large picnic, be especially sure that there'll be plenty of food! Here are some guidelines for estimating the amounts of food you'll need for 10, 25 and 50 servings. The servings listed are average-size; you may need more or less according to the appetites of the guests. For hearty eaters, allow 1½ servings per person, and double the serving size if you'd like enough for seconds.

Food	Serving Size	For 10	For 25	For 50
Beverages				
carbonated	1 (8-oz.) glass	2½ qt.	7 qt.	13 qt.
coffee	1 (6-oz.) cup	¼ lb.	½ lb.	1 lb.
iced tea	1 (12-oz.) glass	4 qt.	10 qt.	20 qt.
lemonade concentrate	1 (8-oz.) glass reconstituted	3 (6-oz.) cans	3 (12-oz.) cans plus 1 (6-oz.) can	6 (12-oz.) cans plus 1 (6-oz.) can
milk	1 (8-oz.) glass	2½ qt.	2 gal.	3½ gal.
punch	1 (6-oz.) serving	2 qt.	5 qt.	10 qt.
Bread	1-oz. slice	1 (1-lb.) loaf	2 (1-lb.) loaves	4 (1-lb.) loaves
Butter	1 tblsp.	½ lb.	1 lb.	1¾ lb.
Casseroles	1 c.	2½ qt.	6¼ qt.	12½ qt.
Cheese				
cottage cheese	½ c.	2½ lb.	6½ lb.	12½ lb.
hard cheese	1 oz.	1 lb.	1½ lb.	3 lb.
Desserts				
cake				
9″ layer	1/12 of 9″ cake	1 cake	2 cakes	4 cakes
13x9x2″ sheet	3″ square	1 cake	2 cakes	4 cakes
ice cream	½ c.	1½ qt.	1 gal.	2 gal.
pie	⅛ of 9″ pie	2 pies	3 pies	6 pies
Fruit				
canned	½ c.	1 (46-oz.) #3 can	1 (104-oz.) #10 can	2 (104-oz.) #10 cans
fresh	1 medium	3 lb.	8 lb.	17 lb.
Meat				
chicken	¼ (3½-lb.) chicken	3 (3½-lb.) chickens	7 (3½-lb.) chickens	13 (3½-lb.) chickens
frankfurters	2 frankfurters	2 lb.	5 to 6 lb.	10 to 12 lb.
ham	4 oz.	2½ lb.	6¼ lb.	12½ lb.
hamburger	4 oz.	2½ lb.	6¼ lb.	12½ lb.
Relishes				
olives	3 to 4	1 pt.	1 qt.	2 qt.
pickles	1 oz.	1 pt.	1 qt.	2 qt.
Salads				
coleslaw, fruit, potato, etc.	½ c.	1½ qt.	3½ qt.	7 qt.
gelatin	½ c.	3 (3-oz.) pkg.	3 (6-oz.) pkg.	6 (6-oz.) pkg.
lettuce salad	⅙ head	2 heads	4-5 heads	8-10 heads
main-dish	1 c.	2½ qt.	6¼ qt.	12½ qt.
Salad Dressings	1 tblsp.	½ pt.	1 pt.	1 qt.
Vegetables				
ears of corn	1 ear	10 ears	25 ears	50 ears
baked potatoes	1 medium	10 medium or 3¼ lb.	25 medium or 8½ lb.	50 medium or 17 lb.

Keeping foods safe

Don't invite salmonellae to your next picnic. These bacteria can cause food poisoning, and they grow rapidly in foods held at temperatures between 44° and 115°F. This type of food poisoning results in headache, vomiting, diarrhea, abdominal cramps and fever, and severe infection can cause death for infants, the elderly and persons with low resistance.

Happily, it's easy to prevent this type of food poisoning. Foods containing mayonnaise, sour cream, eggs, cream, yogurt or fish are particularly hospitable to salmonellae, so during extremely hot, humid weather, it's best not to include these foods in your outdoor menus. A sure-fire way to avoid food poisoning is simple: keep cold foods cold and hot foods hot.

Keeping foods cold

Picnic foods that are usually refrigerated should always be kept cold. Here's how:
• Cool dishes as soon as possible after preparation, and refrigerate until it's time to serve.
• Chill thermal bottles with ice water or place in the refrigerator at least an hour before filling. Foods should stay cold several hours.
• Pack foods in ice chests or coolers. Be sure to add plenty of ice cubes, blocks of ice, crushed ice or sealed refrigerant blocks.
• Count on heavily insulated coolers to keep your food cold for 24 to 48 hours. Inexpensive coolers are fine for shorter periods of time.
• At your picnic site, place coolers in a shady spot covered with a blanket or tarpaulin.

• Open ice chests as seldom as possible after putting foods inside; never let them stand open.

Keeping foods hot

Foods will stay hot for several hours if you pack them carefully. For example:
• Styrofoam or insulated chests can keep foods hot just as well as they can keep foods cold. Wrap thoroughly heated pots of beans, stews or soups in aluminum foil and place in chest. Stuff rolled-up newspaper in the empty spaces and cover tightly; the food will stay hot 2 to 4 hours.
• If you don't have an insulated chest, heat foods thoroughly right in their containers; then wrap in heavy-duty aluminum foil and several layers of newspaper or a terry cloth towel. Place in box or carrier. Foods should stay hot 2 to 4 hours.
• Thermal bottles of all sizes and shapes are available for carrying soups, stews and beverages. Before filling, warm the bottle by filling with boiling water, then drain and refill; the contents will stay hot for hours.

Tips on packing foods

To arrive looking their best, some foods benefit from special handling.

breads (tea)	Cool bread after baking, return to clean loaf pan and cover with aluminum foil.
cakes	Insert wooden picks in top of frosted cake and then cover with a tent of aluminum foil or plastic wrap. (Or carry frosting separately to the site and frost cake just before serving.)
cupcakes (frosted)	Pack in cupcake pan, place a wooden pick in the top of each cupcake and cover loosely with aluminum foil.
deviled eggs	Place stuffed sides together, wrap with plastic wrap and repack in egg carton.
gelatin molds	Keep gelatin in mold and unmold at the picnic table.
mayonnaise	Take only as much as you need for sandwiches and salads; pack in a small jar and keep chilled.
quiche or tart	Keep in its baking pan, invert a slightly larger pan on top and secure with masking tape.
salad greens	Carry chilled greens in covered container and pack the dressing separately.
whipped cream	Carry in a small, chilled container.

Tips for carefree picnicking

• Make a check list of all the foods you plan to take.
• Pack the food just before departure time to help keep hot foods hot and cold foods cold.
• Pack your carryall in reverse order from the way you'll use it, with food on the bottom and tableware on top.
• Place food containers right side up to prevent leaking.
• Arrange foods tightly in carryall so they can't overturn or bump one another.
• Wrap breakable items in several layers of newspaper, kitchen towels or paper towels.
• Take a small first-aid kit containing bandages, insect repellant and sunburn ointment.

Equipping the Outdoor Kitchen

Barbecue grills—charcoal, gas and electric—are manufactured in dozens of sizes and shapes. The three basic styles are open braziers (including hibachis), covered kettle cookers and rectangular covered barbecues. If you plan to buy a grill, your choice depends on how much money you want to spend and how much barbecuing you plan to do.

Barbecue grills

Open braziers are available in a variety of sizes, from tabletop hibachis to large, long-legged units built to cook for a crowd. They're lightweight, inexpensive and easy to use.

A hibachi is just the thing if you don't have room to store a large grill.

These small, efficient grills (single, double and triple-brazier models) come complete with adjustable grates, air dampers, and coal racks to sift down the ashes. Portability is the hibachi's greatest advantage. Since its cooking surface is small, the hibachi is limited to cooking for a few. But you'll save on fuel because just a few coals give off enough heat to cook a meal.

A good brazier has three or four sturdy legs, two with wheels. Some models have removable legs to permit easier transportation and storage when not in use. Other options include half-hoods and rotisseries. Look for a brazier with a removable grill that adjusts easily, and a bowl of heavy metal that won't rust through at the bottom. For added protection, line the bowl with heavy-duty aluminum foil or a bed of sand.

You can use an open brazier for any kind of grilling, although manufacturers don't recommend using it for foods more than two inches thick. Roasts and whole birds can be spit-roasted on an open brazier if you have the proper attachments.

Covered kettle cookers are a little more expensive than open braziers, but are made of more durable materials and are more versatile because they function like an outdoor stove and can be used as either an oven or grill.

With the cover down, there are no open flames, so flare-ups that could char food rarely occur. You also can control the heat by adjusting the dampers in the bowl and in the lid: to lower the heat, close the dampers; if you want a hotter fire, open the dampers to let in more air.

You'll discover that covered cooking is more dependable and faster than open grilling. Since kettle cookers are designed for covered cooking, manufacturers recommend that you do all barbecuing with the lid on.

As a bonus, you can extinguish the fire by closing the dampers and putting on the lid and save the leftover charcoal for your next fire.

Kettle grills vary in size, with an average height of about 40 inches and an average grill diameter of about 20 inches.

Rectangular grills with hinged lids are the most expensive and elaborate grills.

The rectangular or wagon grill is usually constructed of heavy materials, has a hinged lid and offers other options such as warming racks, cutting boards, rotisseries, special oven attachments, convertible grills and built-in fire starters. Some rectangular barbecues are portable, while others are permanently installed on pedestals.

These grills work on the same principle as the covered kettles: the lid turns the barbecue into an oven, and the adjustable dampers allow you to control the fire's temperature. Many models have a built-in thermometer for checking the inside temperature when the lid is closed.

Most manufacturers recommend closing the lid when a constant temperature is required, but fast-cooking foods can be grilled uncovered.

Gas and electric grills are variations of the kettle and rectangular-shaped covered barbecues and use gas or electricity as the heat source instead of charcoal.

Both electric and gas grills save the trouble of building a fire and cleaning up the ashes. Since the preheating time is short, there's little waiting for the grill once the food is ready to cook.

Gas grills and some electric models have volcanic pumice or ceramic briquets that heat up so that when juices drip on them, they produce the smoke that gives food a tantalizing charcoal flavor.

Both gas and electric grills cook food in about the same amount of time as conventional grills. If you have a gas or electric grill, check the manufacturer's directions before using.

Barbecue tools

You'll need only a few tools to simplify barbecuing:
* long-handled tongs—one pair for food and one for coals
* basting brush—choose one made of natural bristles or feathers and use it to brush the grill with oil (to keep foods from sticking) and to baste foods with sauces and marinades
* long-handled turner—handy for turning burgers
* potholders or mitts—for emergency adjustments of the grill
* meat thermometer—not a necessity, but useful for checking the doneness of meat and poultry
* stiff metal brush—to scrub the grill

Using your grill as an oven: Just a few layers of foil can turn a covered grill into an oven. Quick breads, coffee cakes, casseroles and simple desserts will bake perfectly, just as they would in your kitchen range.

The trick is to make a rectangular heat deflector to spread out the heat so the food can bake evenly. You'll need a heat deflector for baking Outdoor Brownies (p. 67), Grill-baked Butterscotch Bars (p. 93), or any one of your own favorite simple bread or dessert recipes. Here's how to make a reusable heat deflector.

Cut 6 sheets of heavy-duty foil the same size as the surface of your grill. (Let's assume your grill is rectangular.)

Place one of these sheets on top of another, and fold in each long edge 1″. Starting at the narrow end, fold foil sheets back and forth, accordian-style. Unfold to within 2″ of the length of the flat sheets.

Place the folded foil on top of two of the flat sheets. Top with remaining two flat sheets, sandwiching the accordian-shaped pieces between the unfolded sheets.

Fold all edges in to secure the folded sheets. The finished deflector should measure 1″ smaller on each side than the surface of the grill (or 2″ smaller than the diameter of a round grill).

Charcoal Cooking Know-How

The real secret of a successful fire is building one that's the right size for the job. You'll need about 30 long-burning briquets for a 20″ grill.

Starting the fire

For some reason, starting a charcoal fire seems to try the patience of even the most experienced outdoor cook.

Generally, the easiest way to start the fire is to stack the briquets in a pyramid. Don't stack them too tightly because good air flow is necessary for lighting. Sprinkle the charcoal with liquid or gel starter and let stand a minute or two before igniting. (Briquets with built-in starter are available, too.) You also may find that an electric starter makes the job a lot easier.

Let the coals burn about 30 minutes or until they've died down to a glow with no areas of black showing. The coals will look pale gray. Most recipes in this book call for cooking over gray coals or medium heat.

Checking the coals

Just extend your hand, palm side down, over the grill approximately where the food will be (about 4 inches from the coals).

Red-gray coals produce the hottest fire used for cooking. You should be able to hold your hand near the grill over this high heat only for about two seconds.

Gray coals produce the medium heat used for most barbecuing, especially foods that are basted with sweet sauces. You'll be able to hold your hand over the coals for about three seconds.

Light gray coals produce low heat and are used for cooking whole birds and large cuts of meat such as roasts. You'll be able to hold your hand over the heat for four or five seconds.

Readying the coals for cooking

Spread the coals into a single layer, using long-handled tongs. The coals should cover an area an inch larger in diameter than the food will be, with the coals touching each other.

If the coals are too hot, wait a little longer. If your grill has dampers, closing them will lower the temperature. If the coals start to get too cool, tap the ashes off the burning coals with tongs and move the coals closer together.

Once the coals are ready, you can

maintain an even temperature by adding five or six new briquets to the fire every half-hour or so. If you keep the briquets on the edge of the grill, they'll warm up and start more easily. Once the fire is burning, never add briquets that have been doused with starter.

Ten tips for charcoal grilling

(For either gas or electric grills, see manufacturer's directions.)
1. Set up the grill on a level spot where there's no draft.
2. Brush grill with cooking oil or spray with nonstick coating to prevent foods from sticking and ease cleanup.
3. Light coals 30 to 40 minutes before you plan to start cooking. The coals are ready for most barbecuing when they look gray (medium heat).
4. Remove meats from the refrigerator or cooler before barbecuing; they'll cook more evenly at room temperature. Allow about 15 minutes for small cuts and an hour for roasts. (If the weather is very hot, don't allow this much time; foods will cook faster on hot days, more slowly on chilly or windy days.)
5. Trim excess fat from meats to prevent sudden flare-ups.
6. Use long-handled tongs, not a fork, to handle and turn meats. (A fork pricks the meat, allowing juices to escape.)
7. Tap coals occasionally to remove ash build-up so fire will keep burning.
8. To prevent burning of meats with sauces containing sugar, begin basting meats toward the end of the cooking time.
9. Keep a water pistol or spray bottle handy to douse flames caused by dripping fat, but don't wet the coals completely.
10. Save partially burned briquets. If you're using a covered grill, lower the lid and close air vents. If you're using

an open brazier, use tongs to transfer hot coals to a metal pail half full of water, then drain and separate the charcoal on a stack of newspapers to dry. Be sure the charcoal is absolutely dry before trying to re-use.

Cleanup

Be sure you've read all the cleaning, care and storage directions supplied with your equipment.

As soon as you've finished barbecuing, cover the grill with wet paper towels or newspapers to let it soak; if you're at home, soak the grill in a sinkful of hot, soapy water while you eat. A stiff metal brush and scouring pads will help loosen large particles.

Let It Rain!

No matter how carefully you plan an outing, sooner or later it'll rain on your picnic or barbecue. If you're caught in a sudden shower in your backyard, move the party indoors—set up a buffet table on the porch or spread a quilt on the living room floor, put on some music, and sit down to eat picnic-style. A garage or barn also makes a fine shelter from the rain, and if you have a picnic table, you can carry it right inside.

If your picnic site is away from home and the skies look gray or even a bit drizzly, pack a tarpaulin or painter's drop cloth to tie between the trees or attach to posts over the picnic table. If you're caught in a real downpour, move back into your car or van for a cozy meal on four wheels, or whisk your guests to a nearby museum or indoor amusement center and enjoy your picnic in a lunchroom or cafeteria. The important thing is to keep the rain from dampening your spirits!

Springtime Celebrations

If you live in an area of the country where the winter weather makes you long for spring, nothing tastes quite as good as that first feast: crisp chicken done to a golden turn, crunchy coleslaw, thick steaks or savory spareribs, sizzling hamburgers and crackly-skinned roasted potatoes.

Steak-lovers are sure to like Grilled Steak Strips (p. 37), a recipe from a Minnesota farm woman who suggests slicing sirloin steak as thin as bacon and marinating it in a soy-flavored sauce. To grill, thread the strips accordian-style on skewers, then eat them just like corn on the cob.

While the meat is grilling over the coals, nibble on whole-wheat crackers or tortilla chips dipped in a colorful Mexican Montage (p. 36), a marvelous concoction of refried beans, sour cream, chopped chilies, alfalfa sprouts and chopped tomatoes. "It's a spectacular hit every time I serve it," writes the Washington farm wife who sent the recipe.

An Ohio farm woman's recipe for London Broil stars in our Mother's Day Barbecue, a menu that takes full advantage of the grill (p. 28). You can heat the Creamy Potato Boats and Buttery Blue Cheese Loaf alongside the beef. For a simple salad, try a Pennsylvania farm woman's recipe for crunchy Broccoli-Egg Salad; it's a refreshing change from mixed green salads, and it's low-calorie, too.

If you're planning a small graduation get-together, try a Stuffed Big Burger with its own homemade sesame seed bun (p. 32). This two-pound hamburger serves up a delicious surprise filling of meltingly good cheese, pickle relish and mustard to eight hungry eaters. A North Carolina farm cook uses a wire grill basket to barbecue this oversized burger, but you can cook it right on the grill and use a baking sheet as a giant spatula.

For lighter fare, try a Texas homemaker's Herbed Chicken Barbecue (p. 22), basted with a lemony marinade, or Chunky Chicken Salad (p. 38), a main dish that can be either sandwiches or salad.

You'll also find dishes that cook in the kitchen, but are easy to carry outdoors to a picnic site. The versatile "Spring Forward" Brunch (p. 12) is perfect for patio entertaining as well as camping because it features a family-sized Potato-Bacon Omelet that can be cooked on a range or over a campfire. The easy Honey-Nut Rolls start with frozen bread dough and can be proofed as usual or in just minutes in a microwave oven.

Everybody's favorite—fried chicken—tastes terrific seasoned with garlic and served in small individual-sized baskets (p. 34). Tuck a Parmesan Cheese Crescent—a golden biscuit-type roll swirled with cheese and parsley—into each basket, too. The Confetti Rice Salad makes a wonderful-looking side dish with its interesting combination of textures and flavors.

These spring menus offer a welcome change from heartier winter fare, and many feature juicy ripe strawberries and other fresh fruits of the season.

Stuffed Mushroom Kabobs*

Steak with Sauce New Orleans*

Cheesy Potato Strips*

Garlic Bread

Peach Upside-down Cake*

Stuffed mushrooms are a great way to begin any get-together. These mushroom kabobs have a spicy sausage stuffing, and cook alongside the Cheesy Potato Strips—which take the longest cooking time. When the mushrooms are ready to serve, the steak will take their place on the grill. The Peach Upside-down Cake tastes best served warm from the oven, so bake it early in the day and warm it on the edge of the grill.

Stuffed Mushroom Kabobs

2 lb. fresh mushrooms
  (1½ to 2" diameter)
1 lb. hot Italian sausage
½ c. chopped onion
1 tsp. dried oregano leaves
1 c. soft bread crumbs
1 (8-oz.) can tomato sauce
cooking oil

IN ADVANCE:
Remove stems from mushrooms, reserving caps. Finely chop stems. Cook stems, sausage, onion and oregano in 10" skillet over medium heat until meat is browned. Remove from heat. Drain fat from skillet.

Stir bread crumbs and tomato sauce into sausage mixture. Set aside.

Fill half of the mushroom caps with the sausage mixture. Top with remaining caps, stem side down. Cover and refrigerate.

TO GRILL:
Thread mushrooms on skewers and grill 4" from gray coals (medium heat). Cook 8 to 10 minutes on each side, basting often with oil. Makes 6 servings.

Steak with Sauce New Orleans

12 oz. beer
½ c. chili sauce
½ c. chopped onion
¼ c. cooking oil
2 tblsp. soy sauce
1 tblsp. Dijon mustard
2 cloves garlic, minced
½ tsp. Tabasco sauce
⅛ tsp. liquid smoke
3 lb. boneless beef sirloin steak, 1½" thick

Combine all ingredients except steak in 3-qt. saucepan. Cook over high heat until mixture comes to a boil. Reduce heat to low and simmer 30 minutes.

Pour sauce into glass bowl, cover and refrigerate.

TO GRILL:

Pour sauce into saucepan and cook over high heat until hot. Brush steak with the hot sauce. Grill steak 4″ from gray coals (medium heat). Cook 10 to 12 minutes on each side, basting often. Serve with remaining sauce. Makes 6 servings.

Cheesy Potato Strips

2 lb. (6 med.) all-purpose potatoes
4 tblsp. butter or regular margarine
¾ c. shredded pasteurized process
  American cheese
6 tblsp. chopped fresh parsley
¼ tsp. salt
⅛ tsp. pepper
¾ c. light cream

IN ADVANCE:

Pare potatoes and cut into ¼″-wide strips. Place in bowl and cover with water. Cover and refrigerate.

TO GRILL:

Drain potatoes thoroughly and pat dry with a paper towel. Place potatoes in an 8″ square baking pan or foil pan. Dot with butter. Sprinkle with cheese, 3 tblsp. of the parsley, salt and pepper. Pour cream over top. Securely wrap entire pan loosely in a 24″ length of heavy-duty foil.

Grill pan 4″ from gray coals (medium heat) for 1 hour to 1 hour 15 minutes. Sprinkle with remaining 3 tblsp. parsley. Makes 6 servings.

Peach Upside-down Cake

⅓ c. butter or regular margarine
⅔ c. brown sugar, packed
2 tblsp. water
1½ c. sliced, pared peaches
1¼ c. sifted flour
¾ c. sugar
1½ tsp. baking powder
½ tsp. salt
⅓ c. shortening
¾ c. milk
1 egg
¼ tsp. almond extract

IN ADVANCE:

Heat butter over low heat in 9″ square baking pan. Remove from heat. Stir in brown sugar and water. Arrange sliced peaches over all. Set aside.

Sift together flour, sugar, baking powder and salt in mixing bowl. Add shortening, milk, egg and almond extract. Beat with an electric mixer at low speed ½ minute. Beat at high speed 3 minutes more. Pour batter into prepared pan.

Bake in 350° oven 45 to 50 minutes or until cake tester or wooden pick inserted in center comes out clean. Cool in pan on rack 5 minutes. Invert pan on rack and remove pan. Cool on rack. Wrap in foil. Makes 6 servings.

TO REHEAT:

Warm foil-wrapped cake on grill.

Minted Grapefruit-Orange Sections*

Potato-Bacon Omelet*

Honey-Nut Rolls*

Homemade Cocoa Mix*

Brunch is a terrific way to entertain, especially during late spring. When you move your clocks forward to daylight-saving time, celebrate the sunlight with a Sunday brunch. Put your serving table on the porch and invite your guests to help themselves from a platter of fresh grapefruit and orange sections while you prepare a big Potato-Bacon Omelet. Our new-fashioned sticky buns start with frozen bread dough that can be proofed in your microwave oven or on your kitchen counter. You'll have lots of cocoa for seconds because it's made from a homemade mix that yields 32 servings.

Minted Grapefruit-Orange Sections

4 oranges
2 pink grapefruit
1 tblsp. chopped fresh mint leaves
  or ½ tsp. dried mint leaves
romaine lettuce leaves

IN ADVANCE:
Peel oranges and grapefruit with a sharp knife, removing the white part of peel. Cut into sections. Sprinkle with mint. Toss lightly to mix well. Cover and refrigerate until ready to serve.
TO SERVE:
Place lettuce leaves on salad plates. Top with an equal amount of fruit mixture. Makes 6 servings.

Potato-Bacon Omelet

8 strips bacon
1½ c. diced, pared potatoes
3 tblsp. chopped onion
1½ tsp. salt
3 tblsp. chopped fresh parsley
2 tblsp. chopped pimientos
2 tblsp. cooking oil
12 eggs, beaten
2 tblsp. water
¼ tsp. pepper

Fry bacon until crisp in 10″ skillet. Remove and drain on paper towels. Crumble. Reserve 2 tblsp. bacon fat. Add potatoes, onion and ½ tsp. of the salt to reserved fat. Cook until potatoes are tender and golden. Stir in parsley, pimientos, and bacon; set aside.

Heat oil in 12″ skillet over medium heat. Beat together eggs, water, remaining 1 tsp. salt and pepper. Stir in vegetable mixture; pour into skillet. With fork, lift cooked edges so uncooked portion flows underneath. Slide pan back and forth to avoid sticking. Cook until mixture is set, but top is creamy. Fold in half and slide onto serving platter. Makes 6 servings.

Honey-Nut Rolls

1 (1-lb.) loaf frozen bread dough
¼ c. butter or regular margarine
¼ c. honey
⅓ c. chopped walnuts

Let dough thaw at room temperature. Cut loaf into 12 slices and set aside.

Combine butter and honey in 1-qt. saucepan. Cook over medium heat until butter is melted. Pour into greased 8″ round glass baking dish. Sprinkle with walnuts.

Dip each slice of bread dough in butter mixture and arrange in the same baking dish. Cover and let rise until doubled, about 30 minutes.

Bake in 350° oven 25 minutes or until golden brown. Invert onto serving plate and serve hot. Makes 12 rolls.

VARIATION: To thaw and proof dough using a microwave oven, lightly grease surface of frozen loaf and place dough on a dish. Place dish on an inverted saucer in the microwave oven. Cover with waxed paper and microwave (medium setting) 2½ minutes, rotating dish one-half turn after each minute.

Proceed as above, dipping slices of dough into butter mixture. Arrange slices in baking dish and place dish on an inverted saucer in the microwave oven. Cover surface of dough with waxed paper and microwave (medium setting) 3 to 4 minutes, rotating dish after each minute until dough is doubled.

Bake as directed above.

Homemade Cocoa Mix

3 c. sifted confectioners' sugar
3 c. nonfat dry milk
2 c. miniature marshmallows
1 c. powdered non-dairy creamer
1 c. baking cocoa
hot milk

IN ADVANCE:
Combine confectioners' sugar, nonfat dry milk, marshmallows, creamer and cocoa in bowl. Mix well. Spoon into airtight container and cover. Makes 8 c. mix, enough for 32 (8-oz.) servings when milk is added.

TO SERVE:
Place ¼ c. cocoa mix in cup. Stir in ¾ c. hot milk and mix until well blended.

ALFRESCO AMERICAN-STYLE

Oven-style Rib Barbecue*

Macaroni-Fruit Salad*

Brown Sugar Tea Bread*

Pears in Mint Sauce*

Celebrate the change of season by dining alfresco. Each recipe in this menu is prepared indoors, but can be enjoyed under the open sky as soon as weather permits. Oven-style Rib Barbecue has a tomato-based sauce spiked with chili powder. For a cool contrast, Macaroni-Fruit Salad offers fruit, whipped cream and miniature marshmallows—a sweet new twist for a macaroni salad. The round loaves of Brown Sugar Tea Bread are baked in one-pound coffee cans and need neither eggs nor shortening. Top off the meal with a simple dessert of thinly sliced pears in a mint sauce garnished with juicy blackberries—or your favorite fresh fruit.

Oven-style Rib Barbecue

2 c. ketchup
½ c. brown sugar, packed
½ c. vinegar
2 tblsp. Worcestershire sauce
2 tsp. chili powder
½ tsp. salt
½ tsp. Tabasco sauce
6 lb. pork spareribs, cut up
3 medium onions, sliced

IN ADVANCE:
   Combine ketchup, brown sugar, vinegar, Worcestershire sauce, chili powder, salt and Tabasco sauce in glass bowl. Mix well. Cover and refrigerate.
TO COOK:
   Arrange ribs in shallow roasting pan; cover with onions. Pour half of sauce over ribs. Cover with foil.
   Bake in 350° oven 1½ hours. Uncover, baste with remaining sauce and bake 30 minutes more or until tender. Makes 6 to 8 servings.

Macaroni-Fruit Salad

8 oz. macaroni twists
1 (8-oz.) can crushed pineapple
water
½ c. sugar
1 egg
1 tblsp. flour
⅛ tsp. salt
1 (8½-oz.) can fruit cocktail, drained
1 c. miniature marshmallows
¼ c. halved maraschino cherries
1 c. heavy cream, whipped

IN ADVANCE:
   Cook macaroni according to package directions for salads.
   Drain pineapple and reserve juice.

Add enough water to juice to make ½ c. Combine ½ c. juice, sugar, eggs, flour and salt in 1-qt. saucepan.

Cook over medium heat, stirring constantly, until mixture thickens and coats a metal spoon. Remove from heat.

Combine macaroni and egg mixture in bowl. Toss lightly but well. Cover and refrigerate at least 4 hours.

Fold fruit cocktail, marshmallows, maraschino cherries and pineapple into chilled macaroni mixture. Then gently fold in whipped cream. Cover and refrigerate several hours before serving. Makes 6 c. or 6 to 8 servings.

Brown Sugar Tea Bread

2½ c. coffee (fresh-perked, instant
* or leftover)*
1½ c. raisins
4 tsp. baking soda
4 c. sifted flour
2 c. brown sugar, packed
2 c. chopped walnuts
1 tblsp. grated orange rind
1 tblsp. ground cinnamon
½ tsp. salt

IN ADVANCE:

Heat coffee in 2-qt. saucepan over high heat to a boil. Remove from heat. Add raisins and baking soda. Let stand for 30 minutes. Add flour, brown sugar, walnuts, orange rind, cinnamon and salt, stirring just enough to moisten.

Pour an equal amount of mixture into each of 3 greased and floured (1-lb.) coffee cans (cans will be slightly more than half full).

Bake in 325° oven 65 minutes or until tester inserted in center comes out clean. Cool in cans on rack 15 minutes. Remove from cans; cool slightly. Serve

warm; or cool completely, wrap in foil and refrigerate until ready to serve. Makes 3 loaves.

TO REHEAT:

Place foil-wrapped loaves in 350° oven 10 minutes.

Pears in Mint Sauce

Mint Sauce (recipe follows)
8 pears, pared and thinly sliced
1 c. fresh blackberries or blueberries

IN ADVANCE:

Prepare Mint Sauce. Dip pear slices in Mint Sauce. Refrigerate in covered container about 2 hours.

TO SERVE:

Spoon pear slices into dessert dishes and garnish with fresh blackberries. Makes 8 servings.

MINT SAUCE: Combine 1½ c. sugar and 2 tblsp. cornstarch in 2-qt. saucepan. Stir in ½ c. light corn syrup and 2 c. water. Cook over medium heat until mixture comes to a boil. Boil 3 minutes or until mixture is clear and slightly syrupy. Remove from heat; stir in 2 tblsp. lemon juice, 1 tsp. peppermint extract and 12 drops green food coloring. Cool to room temperature.

Bologna-Pickle Spread*

Whole-wheat Buns*

Fresh Fruit Slush*

Jumbo Oatmeal-Peanut Butter Cookies*

Every farmer is familiar with the four o'clock slump—the tired feeling that comes just when the pressure is on to finish that field before dark. So if you're planning an afternoon of hard work outdoors, plan to take a break with a picnic hamper of high-protein snacks. Both men and youngsters will like the combination of bologna and cheese on homemade Whole-wheat Buns, and even the cookies provide a quick energy boost.

Bologna-Pickle Spread

1½ lb. regular bologna, ground
   (about 4½ c.)
¾ c. pickle relish
3 tblsp. minced onion
1 tblsp. Worcestershire sauce
1½ c. salad dressing
12 Whole-wheat Buns (recipe follows)
12 slices pasteurized process
   American cheese
lettuce leaves

IN ADVANCE:
   Combine bologna, pickle relish, onion, Worcestershire sauce and salad dressing. Mix well. Cover and refrigerate. Makes ½ c.
TO SERVE:
   Split Whole-wheat Buns. Using about ⅓ c. for each sandwich, spread bologna mixture on buns. Top each bun with a cheese slice and a lettuce leaf. Makes 12 sandwiches.

Whole-wheat Buns

2 c. water
½ c. sugar
½ c. nonfat dry milk
1 tblsp. salt
¾ c. cooking oil
4½ to 5 c. sifted flour (all-purpose)
2 pkg. active dry yeast
3 eggs
3½ c. stirred whole wheat flour
milk

IN ADVANCE:
   Combine water, sugar, dry milk, salt and oil in 2-qt. saucepan. Heat over low heat to very warm (120 to 130°).
   Stir together 4 c. of the all-purpose

flour and undissolved yeast in bowl. Add very warm liquid and eggs. Beat with an electric mixer at low speed ½ minute, scraping sides of bowl constantly. Beat at high speed 3 minutes more, scraping bowl occasionally.

Stir in whole-wheat flour by hand. Add enough remaining all-purpose flour to make a moderately soft dough. Turn dough out onto floured surface. Knead until smooth and elastic, about 5 minutes.

Place in greased bowl, turning to grease top. Cover and let rise in warm place until doubled, about 1 to 1½ hours.

Punch down dough. Divide into thirds. Cover and let rest 10 minutes.

Divide each third into 8 portions. Shape into balls. Place on greased baking sheets about 3″ apart. Press down with palm of hand to make 3½″ rounds. Cover and let rise in warm place until doubled, 30 to 45 minutes. Brush with milk.

Bake in 375° oven 12 minutes or until golden brown. Remove from baking sheets. Cool on racks. Wrap any leftover buns in foil and freeze. Makes 24 buns.

Fresh Fruit Slush

4 large oranges
2 c. sliced fresh strawberries
1 c. seedless green grapes
3 medium bananas, sliced
1 (6-oz.) can frozen lemonade concentrate, slightly thawed

IN ADVANCE:
Peel oranges with a sharp knife, removing all of the white part of peel. Cut sections from membrane and place sections in bowl. Squeeze membrane over same bowl to release juices. Add strawberries, grapes, bananas and lemonade. Toss lightly to mix well.

Spoon into cups, cover with aluminum foil and refrigerate.

About 1 to 1¼ hours before serving, place fruit cups in freezer. Freeze until slightly icy. Makes about 8 c. or 12 servings.

Jumbo Oatmeal-Peanut Butter Cookies

2 c. sifted flour
1 tsp. baking soda
1 tsp. salt
1 tsp. ground cinnamon
¾ c. butter or regular margarine
½ c. peanut butter
1 c. sugar
1 c. brown sugar, packed
2 eggs
¼ c. milk
1 tsp. vanilla
1½ c. quick-cooking oats
1 c. raisins

IN ADVANCE:
Sift together flour, baking soda, salt and cinnamon; set aside.

Cream together butter, peanut butter, sugar and brown sugar in bowl until light and fluffy, using an electric mixer at medium speed. Add eggs, one at a time, beating well after each addition. Blend in milk and vanilla.

Gradually stir dry ingredients into creamed mixture, blending well. Stir in oats and raisins. Drop mixture by tablespoonfuls, about 2″ apart, on greased baking sheets.

Bake in 350° oven 15 minutes or until done. Makes 36 (3″) cookies.

Cornish Hens à l'Orange*

Cantonese-style Vegetables*

Pineapple-Cheese Ring*

Banana Split Pie*

For those times when only *something special will do, let Cornish Hens à l'Orange head your menu. You can picnic at home elegantly with these hens, which are stuffed with a light, orange-flavored pilaf and roasted on a spit. Frequent basting gives the crispy browned hens a beautiful glaze. Cantonese-style Vegetables, cooked in a skillet till they're just tender-crisp, are a wonderful combination of textures and flavors. Serve Pineapple-Cheese Ring on a bed of fresh greens as a separate course or as a side dish. Almost everyone loves a banana split, and just about everyone will enjoy Banana Split Pie, a concoction of ice cream and bananas in a crunchy meringue shell.*

Cornish Hens à l'Orange

2 c. orange juice
1 c. uncooked regular rice
3 tblsp. chopped green pepper
3 tblsp. chopped onion
3 tblsp. chopped celery
3 tblsp. raisins
½ tsp. salt
½ tsp. grated orange rind
3 tblsp. chopped walnuts
6 (1-lb.) cornish hens
½ c. orange marmalade, melted

IN ADVANCE:

Heat orange juice in a 3-qt. saucepan over high heat until mixture comes to a boil. Stir in rice, green pepper, onion, celery, raisins, salt and orange rind; return to a boil. Reduce heat to low.

Cover and simmer 15 minutes or until liquid is absorbed. Remove from heat; stir in walnuts. Cover and refrigerate.

TO GRILL:

Loosely stuff cavity of each hen with rice mixture. Close cavities and secure with wooden picks. Run spit crosswise through the center of each hen. Set spit forks in hens on both ends and tighten. Holding spit at both ends, turn. If any hen drops downward, adjust hen so it is balanced.

Place on grill rotisserie; close lid and grill over light gray coals (low heat), basting often with orange marmalade. Cook 1 hour or until tender and the juices run clear. Makes 6 servings.

Cantonese-style Vegetables

¼ c. cooking oil
2 c. French-cut green beans, fresh or frozen
1 (6-oz.) can water chestnuts, thinly sliced
½ lb. fresh mushrooms, sliced
1 medium green pepper, cut into strips

1 c. diagonally sliced celery
¾ tsp. salt
½ tsp. garlic salt
¼ tsp. pepper
1 (10½-oz.) can condensed chicken broth
2 tblsp. cornstarch
1 (4-oz.) jar pimientos, drained and diced
⅓ c. toasted slivered almonds

Heat oil in 12″ skillet and add green beans, water chestnuts, mushrooms, green pepper, celery, salt, garlic salt and pepper. Cook, stirring frequently, for about 10 minutes or until vegetables are tender-crisp.

Add enough water to broth to make 1½ c. Combine broth and cornstarch; stir to blend. Add to vegetable mixture and cook until thickened. Add pimientos. Serve topped with almonds. Makes 6 servings.

Pineapple-Cheese Ring

2 (8-oz.) cans crushed pineapple
1 (3-oz.) pkg. lemon-flavored gelatin
½ c. boiling water
1 c. heavy cream, whipped
1 c. creamed small-curd cottage cheese
1 c. finely chopped celery
½ c. chopped walnuts

IN ADVANCE:
Drain pineapple, reserving ½ c. of the juice. Combine gelatin and boiling water in bowl, stirring constantly until gelatin is completely dissolved. Stir in reserved ½ c. pineapple juice.

Refrigerate 45 to 60 minutes or until partially set.

Using an electric mixer at high speed, beat gelatin mixture until light and foamy. Fold into whipped cream. Fold in cottage cheese, celery and walnuts. Pour into lightly oiled 6-cup ring mold.

Refrigerate several hours or until set.
TO SERVE:
Unmold by wrapping a cloth dipped

in warm water around mold, invert onto serving plate and shake gently. Makes 6 to 10 servings.

Banana Split Pie

3 egg whites
¼ tsp. cream of tartar
¾ c. sugar
¾ tsp. vanilla
3 tblsp. baking cocoa
baked 9″ pie shell
1 c. heavy cream
1 tblsp. sugar
½ tsp. vanilla
1 qt. strawberry ice cream
½ c. strawberry ice cream topping
2 medium bananas, sliced

IN ADVANCE:
Beat together egg whites and cream of tartar in bowl until foamy, using an electric mixer at high speed. Gradually add ¾ c. sugar, 1 tblsp. at a time, beating well after each addition. Continue beating until stiff, glossy peaks form. Beat in ¾ tsp. vanilla.

Add cocoa, a little at a time, folding a few strokes after each addition. Spread meringue in bottom and up sides of baked pie shell.

Bake in 325° oven 25 minutes or until meringue is set, but still slightly soft. Cool on rack.
TO SERVE:
Just before serving, combine heavy cream, 1 tblsp. sugar and ½ tsp. vanilla in chilled bowl. Beat until soft peaks form, using an electric mixer at high speed; set aside.

Spoon half of the ice cream into meringue-lined pie shell. Top with strawberry topping. Spoon remaining ice cream over topping. Arrange bananas on top. Spread sweetened whipped cream over pie. Serve immediately. Makes 6 to 8 servings.

Pizza Burgers*

Danish Potato Salad*

Fruit Kabobs*

Choco-Mint Ice Cream Sodas*

Many outdoor chefs specialize in burgers and potato salad. Pizza Burgers—hamburgers flavored with pepperoni and mozzarella cheese—are an easy change of pace. Slices of pepperoni in the center of each patty flavor the beef in every bite. Danish Potato Salad is bathed in an extra-creamy cooked dressing. Colorful Fruit Kabobs, chunks of fresh fruit alternated on skewers, are grilled and basted with a ginger-flavored butter sauce. Cool off with old-fashioned ice cream sodas made doubly flavorful with chocolate and peppermint.

Pizza Burgers

2 lb. ground beef
1½ tsp. salt
½ tsp. dried oregano leaves
¼ tsp. pepper
¼ c. tomato sauce
2 oz. sliced pepperoni
6 green pepper rings
3 slices mozzarella cheese, cut in half
6 hamburger buns

IN ADVANCE:

Combine ground beef, salt, oregano and pepper in bowl. Mix lightly, but well. Divide mixture into 12 equal portions. Shape each portion into a thin patty. Spoon an equal amount of tomato sauce and pepperoni on top of each of 6 patties.

Place remaining patties on top and press edges together to seal well. Cover and refrigerate.

TO GRILL:

Cook patties 4" from gray coals (medium heat) 4 to 5 minutes. Turn, top with green pepper ring and half of a slice of cheese. Cook 4 to 5 minutes more. Serve on hamburger buns. Makes 6 servings.

Danish Potato Salad

4 c. cubed, cooked potatoes (about 2 lb.)
2 hard-cooked eggs, chopped
½ c. chopped cucumbers
1 tblsp. minced onion
1 tblsp. chopped green pepper
¼ c. vinegar
¼ c. water
¼ c. sugar
1 tsp. prepared mustard
¼ tsp. salt

¹/₁₆ tsp. pepper
2 eggs, well beaten
1 c. salad dressing

IN ADVANCE:

Combine potatoes, hard-cooked eggs, cucumber, onion and green pepper in bowl. Set aside.

Combine vinegar, water, sugar, prepared mustard, salt and pepper in 2-qt. saucepan. Cook over high heat until mixture comes to a boil. Reduce heat to medium; gradually beat in eggs. Cook, stirring constantly, about 5 minutes until slightly thickened. Beat in salad dressing.

Pour dressing mixture over potato mixture. Toss lightly to mix well. Adjust seasonings if necessary. Cover and refrigerate until ready to serve. Makes 4½ c. or 6 servings.

VARIATION: To make 6 qt., increase ingredients to 10 lb. diced, cooked potatoes, 6 hard-cooked eggs (chopped), 2 c. chopped cucumber, ½ c. minced onion, ½ c. chopped green pepper, 1 c. vinegar, 1 c. water, 1 c. sugar, 1 tblsp. prepared mustard, 1 tsp. salt, ½ tsp. pepper, 5 eggs (well beaten) and 1 qt. salad dressing. Proceed as above. Makes 32 servings.

Fruit Kabobs

1 fresh pineapple
2 large oranges, unpeeled
¾ c. butter or regular margarine
3 tblsp. sugar
1¾ tsp. ground ginger
3 apples
24 maraschino cherries

IN ADVANCE:

Pare and cut pineapple into 1″ cubes. Place in bowl. Cut oranges into ¾″

slices. Place in bowl with pineapple. Cover and refrigerate.

TO GRILL:

Combine butter, sugar and ginger in 1-qt. saucepan. Heat over low heat until butter is melted. Remove from heat; keep warm. Meanwhile, core and cut apples into 1″ cubes.

Alternately thread pineapple, oranges, apples and cherries on 6 (12″) skewers. Grill kabobs 4″ from gray coals (medium heat), turning and basting often with butter sauce. Cook 10 to 12 minutes or until lightly browned and glazed. Makes 6 servings.

Choco-Mint Ice Cream Sodas

¾ c. chocolate-flavored syrup
¼ tsp. peppermint extract
1½ qt. club soda, chilled
1½ c. milk
1 qt. mint-chocolate chip ice cream

Combine chocolate syrup and peppermint extract in bowl; mix well.

Spoon 2 tblsp. chocolate syrup mixture into each of 6 (16-oz.) glasses. Pour ½ c. club soda and ¼ c. milk into each glass. Stir until well blended. Add 2 scoops of ice cream to each glass. Gradually pour ½ c. more club soda into each glass. Stir. Serve with iced beverage spoons and straws. Makes 6 servings.

Herbed Chicken Barbecue*

Low-Cal Scalloped Potatoes*

Barbecue Slaw*

Whole-wheat Batter Bread*

Next time you plan to cook chicken on the grill, break the routine of spicy, red-sauced barbecue with the savory taste of *Herbed Chicken Barbecue*. Marinate the chicken for several hours in a mildly seasoned blend of lemon and herbs, then grill it to a golden brown over the coals. These *Low-Cal Scalloped Potatoes* are a full-flavored, slimmed-down version with skim milk substituting for whole milk or cream. They'll bake in the oven while the chicken cooks outdoors; or they can be cooked in advance and carried to your picnic site.

Herbed Chicken Barbecue

1 c. cooking oil
½ c. lemon juice
2 tsp. salt
2 tsp. dried basil leaves
1 tsp. paprika
1 tsp. minced onion
½ tsp. dried thyme leaves
1 clove garlic, minced
2 (2½ to 3-lb.) broiler-fryers, cut up

IN ADVANCE:

Combine oil, lemon juice, salt, basil, paprika, onion, thyme and garlic in a jar. Cover and shake until well blended. Arrange chicken in 13x9x2" (3-qt.) glass baking dish. Pour marinade over chicken.

Cover and refrigerate at least 6 hours or overnight, turning occasionally.

TO GRILL:

Cook chicken 4" from gray coals (medium heat), turning and basting often with marinade. Cook 1 hour or until tender. Makes 8 servings.

Low-Cal Scalloped Potatoes

2 lb. potatoes, pared and thinly sliced
  (about 5 c.)
1 c. thinly sliced onion
2 tblsp. flour
1 tsp. salt
1/8 tsp. pepper
1 c. skim milk, scalded
1 c. chicken broth
paprika

Arrange one-third of the potatoes in a lightly greased 2-qt. casserole. Arrange one-third of the onion on top of the potatoes. Combine flour, salt and pepper in bowl. Sprinkle one-third of the flour mixture over potatoes and onion. Repeat layers twice.

Pour hot milk and chicken broth over all. Sprinkle with paprika.

Bake in 375° oven 1½ hours. Uncover and bake 30 minutes more or until potatoes are tender. Makes 8 servings.

Barbecue Slaw

1 medium cabbage, shredded (about 10 c.)
2 large green peppers, chopped
1 (16-oz.) can tomatoes, cut up
2 c. sweet mixed pickles, drained
  and chopped
¼ c. chopped onion
½ c. sugar
¼ c. vinegar
1 tblsp. salt
¼ tsp. pepper

IN ADVANCE:

Combine cabbage, green peppers, tomatoes, pickles and onion in glass bowl. Set aside.

Combine sugar, vinegar, salt and pep-per in another bowl. Mix well. Pour over cabbage mixture. Toss lightly to mix well.

Cover and refrigerate until ready to serve. Makes 8 servings.

Whole-wheat Batter Bread

2½ c. stirred whole-wheat flour
½ c. wheat germ
⅓ c. nonfat dry milk
2 pkg. active dry yeast
2 tsp. salt
⅓ c. molasses
2 tblsp. shortening
2 c. very warm water (120 to 130°)
2½ c. sifted flour (all-purpose)

IN ADVANCE:

Stir together 1½ c. of the whole-wheat flour, wheat germ, dry milk, yeast and salt in a bowl. Add molasses, shortening and very warm water. Beat 2 minutes, using an electric mixer at high speed.

Stir in remaining 1 c. whole-wheat flour and enough all-purpose flour to make a soft dough. Cover; let rise in warm place until doubled, about 40 minutes.

Stir down dough. Turn into greased 2-qt. soufflé dish or casserole. Cover; let rise until dough is level with top of dish, about 15 minutes.

Bake in 400° oven 20 minutes. Cover with foil; bake 20 minutes more or until browned. Remove from casserole. Serve immediately; or cool completely and wrap in foil until ready to serve. Makes 1 loaf.

TO REHEAT:

Warm foil-wrapped bread on grill, or place in 375° oven 10 minutes.

Pork Chops
with Orange-Apple Stuffing*

Green Beans with Almonds*

Garlic Bubble Loaf*

Pina Colada Flip*

The Illinois farm woman who shared this recipe for Pork Chops with Orange-Apple Stuffing says it makes an impressive company dish. The fruity stuffing complements the flavor of the pork, and the chops are basted with orange juice as they cook. Green Beans with Almonds cook in a foil packet right on the grill. We teamed the meat and vegetables with a Nebraska farm wife's recipe for rich and buttery Garlic Bubble Loaf, a shortcut recipe for a pull-apart loaf of bread which gets its name from its shape—portions of dough rolled into "bubbles" in the palms of your hands. For a festive dessert, fill your punch bowl with the ingredients for Pina Colada Flip adding ice cream and club soda just before serving.

Pork Chops with Orange-Apple Stuffing

6 pork chops, 1″ thick
salt
pepper
1½ c. toasted raisin bread cubes
  (½″ cubes)
1 tsp. grated orange rind
1 orange, peeled, sectioned and chopped
1 egg
¼ tsp. salt
⅛ tsp. ground cinnamon
2 tblsp. butter or regular margarine
½ c. chopped celery
1 medium apple, unpared and chopped
½ c. orange juice

IN ADVANCE:

Using a sharp knife, slit chops open, cutting from fat side almost to bone to form a pocket. Sprinkle salt and pepper in pocket. Cover and refrigerate until ready to cook.

Combine bread cubes, orange rind, orange, egg, ¼ tsp. salt and cinnamon in a bowl. Mix lightly, but well. Set aside.

Heat butter over medium heat in 1-qt. saucepan until melted. Add celery and apple and sauté until tender but not brown. Remove from heat.

Pour celery and apple mixture over bread mixture. Mix lightly, but well. Cover and refrigerate.

TO GRILL:

Stuff each pork chop with about ¼ c. stuffing, and secure with wooden picks. Grill chops 4″ from gray coals (medium heat), turning and basting often with orange juice. Cook 1 hour or until no longer pink in center. Makes 6 servings.

Green Beans with Almonds

2 lb. fresh green beans
1 tsp. salt
¼ tsp. pepper
4 tblsp. butter or regular margarine
¼ c. toasted, slivered almonds

IN ADVANCE:

Remove tips and strings from green beans. Place beans on a 24″ length of heavy-duty foil and sprinkle with salt and pepper. Top with butter. Securely wrap mixture into a loose packet and refrigerate.

TO GRILL:

Cook bean packet 4″ from gray coals (medium heat) 20 minutes, turning once after 10 minutes. To serve, sprinkle with almonds. Makes 6 servings.

Garlic Bubble Loaf

⅓ c. butter or regular margarine
2 cloves garlic, minced
1 (1-lb.) loaf frozen bread dough, thawed
½ c. grated Parmesan cheese

IN ADVANCE:

Heat butter over medium heat in 1-qt. saucepan until melted. Sauté garlic in butter until tender but not browned. Remove from heat.

Cut thawed dough in half lengthwise and cut each half into 12 pieces. Shape each piece into a ball. Roll balls in butter mixture; then roll in Parmesan cheese. Place coated balls in well-greased 9x5x3″ loaf pan. Pour any remaining butter mixture and cheese over top of balls.

Cover and let rise in warm place until almost doubled, about 30 minutes.

Bake in 350° oven 20 to 25 minutes or until browned. Remove from pan and serve immediately; or cool completely on rack, wrap in foil and refrigerate until ready to serve. Makes 1 loaf, about 6 servings.

TO REHEAT:

Warm foil-wrapped bread on grill.

Pina Colada Flip

1 (46-oz.) can pineapple juice, chilled
1 (16-oz.) can cream of coconut
1 qt. vanilla ice cream
1 (28-oz.) bottle club soda, chilled

IN ADVANCE:

Combine pineapple juice and cream of coconut in punch bowl. Mix well. Cover and refrigerate.

TO SERVE:

Spoon ice cream into chilled pineapple mixture. Slowly pour in club soda. Makes about 3 qt. or about 6 (16-oz.) servings.

Stuffed Lamb Breast*

Grilled Potatoes au Gratin*

Buttered Peas

Pickled Carrots*

Strawberry-Rhubarb Crisp*

Tender young lamb plays a starring role on many indoor menus, but *Stuffed Lamb Breast* is a great choice for barbecuing, too. Chock-full of a savory bread stuffing flecked with shredded carrot, this version is glazed with currant jelly and served with *Grilled Potatoes au Gratin* and piquant *Pickled Carrots*. For dessert, we've paired two other seasonal flavors in a rosy *Strawberry-Rhubarb Crisp*.

Stuffed Lamb Breast

6 tblsp. butter or regular margarine
1½ c. shredded, pared carrots
½ c. chopped onion
4 c. bread cubes (½")
½ c. chicken broth
¼ c. chopped fresh parsley
½ tsp. dried savory leaves
½ tsp. salt
⅛ tsp. pepper
2 (2-lb.) breasts of lamb
½ c. currant jelly, melted

IN ADVANCE:

Heat butter in a 10" skillet over low heat until melted. Sauté carrots and onion in butter until tender but not browned. Add bread cubes, chicken broth, parsley, savory, salt and pepper. Toss lightly to mix well. Remove from heat. Spoon mixture into bowl. Cover and refrigerate.

TO GRILL:

Using a sharp knife, cut pocket in each lamb breast and trim away as much fat as possible. Lightly stuff each pocket with half of the bread-vegetable mixture; close openings with skewers or sew with thread.

Grill 4" from gray coals (medium heat) 1 hour or to desired doneness, turning often and basting with melted jelly during the last 20 minutes of cooking. Makes 6 servings.

Grilled Potatoes au Gratin

5 bacon strips, cooked, drained
  and crumbled
½ c. shredded Cheddar cheese
¼ c. chopped onion
7 c. sliced, pared potatoes
½ tsp. salt
⅛ tsp. pepper
½ c. butter or regular margarine, melted

IN ADVANCE:

Combine bacon, cheese and onion in bowl. Cover and refrigerate.

TO GRILL:

Arrange potatoes on a 24″ length of heavy-duty foil and sprinkle with salt and pepper. Sprinkle bacon mixture evenly over potatoes. Drizzle butter over top. Securely wrap mixture into a loose packet.

Grill 4″ from gray coals (medium heat) 1 hour or until tender. Makes 6 servings.

Pickled Carrots

1½ c. water
2 lb. carrots, pared and sliced
1 (10½-oz.) can condensed tomato soup
1 c. sugar
¾ c. wine vinegar
½ c. cooking oil
1 tsp. salt
1 tsp. prepared mustard
1 tsp. Worcestershire sauce
¼ tsp. pepper
½ c. chopped green pepper
1 (3½-oz.) jar cocktail onions, drained
1 small head iceberg lettuce

IN ADVANCE:

Heat water in 3-qt. saucepan over high heat until it comes to a boil. Add carrots; return water to a boil and cook, uncovered, 12 minutes or until tender. Drain carrots and plunge into a bowl of ice water. Set aside.

Meanwhile, combine soup, sugar, wine vinegar, oil, salt, mustard, Worcestershire sauce and pepper in bowl; blend well. Set aside. Drain carrots and combine with green pepper and onions in glass bowl.

Pour marinade over vegetables. Cover and refrigerate at least 2 days.

TO SERVE:

Carefully remove 6 leaves from head of lettuce. Lettuce leaves will form a cup. Drain vegetables and spoon into lettuce cups. Makes 6 servings.

Strawberry-Rhubarb Crisp

2 lb. fresh rhubarb
1 (3-oz.) pkg. strawberry-flavored gelatin
½ c. unsifted flour
½ c. sugar
½ c. brown sugar, packed
½ tsp. ground cinnamon
¼ c. butter or regular margarine, melted

IN ADVANCE:

Wash rhubarb; cut off and discard leaves. Cut stalks into ¾″ pieces (5 c.). Arrange rhubarb in greased 8″ square glass baking dish. Sprinkle with strawberry-flavored gelatin; set aside.

Combine flour, sugar, brown sugar and cinnamon in bowl. Add butter and mix until crumbly. Sprinkle over rhubarb.

Bake in 350° oven 50 minutes or until rhubarb is tender. Let stand at least 30 minutes before serving. Makes 6 servings.

London Broil*

Creamy Potato Boats*

Broccoli-Egg Salad*

Buttery Blue Cheese Loaf*

Strawberries and Cream

Honor Mom with an afternoon outdoors (and out of the kitchen!). Ask Dad to ready the grill while the rest of the family begins the food preparation. Broccoli-Egg Salad, assembled indoors, is an easy and interesting way to serve raw broccoli. Creamy Potato Boats—a blend of mashed potatoes, cream cheese and herbs—are heated on the grill in individual foil packets alongside the London Broil. When the meat is turned, place foil-wrapped Buttery Blue Cheese Loaf on the edge of the grill to warm.

London Broil

¼ c. cooking oil
2 tblsp. lemon juice
2 tblsp. soy sauce
2 tblsp. chopped green onion
1 clove garlic, minced
1 tsp. pepper
1 tsp. celery salt
2 to 2½ lb. beef flank steak or
   London broil, 1" thick

IN ADVANCE:
Combine oil, lemon juice, soy sauce, green onion, garlic, pepper and celery salt in 12x8x2" (2-qt.) glass baking dish. Mix well.

Score steak on both sides. Add steak to marinade, turning to coat both sides. Cover and refrigerate overnight, turning occasionally.

TO GRILL:
Cook steak 6" from red coals (high heat). Grill 10 to 12 minutes on each side or to desired doneness, basting often with marinade.

TO SERVE:
Cut diagonally into very thin slices. Makes 6 servings.

Creamy Potato Boats

2½ lb. all-purpose potatoes, pared
   and quartered
1 tsp. salt
water
1 (3-oz.) pkg. cream cheese with chives,
   cubed
2 tblsp. butter or regular margarine
¼ tsp. garlic salt
⅛ tsp. pepper
1 c. heavy cream
paprika
1 tblsp. butter or regular margarine

Place potatoes in 4-qt. Dutch oven with ½ tsp. of the salt and enough water to cover. Cover and cook over high heat until water comes to a boil. Reduce heat to low and simmer 30 minutes or until tender. Drain well.

Mash potatoes with a potato masher until smooth. Add cream cheese, 2 tblsp. butter, garlic salt, pepper and remaining ½ tsp. salt. Mix until smooth. Gradually add heavy cream, mixing until smooth after each addition.

Divide potato mixture into 6 portions and place each portion on a 12″ square of heavy-duty foil. Shape into boat-shaped mounds. Sprinkle each with paprika and dot with ½ tsp. butter. Wrap securely and refrigerate.

TO GRILL:

Cook potato packets 6″ from red coals (high heat). Cook 20 to 24 minutes or until hot, rearranging packets occasionally. Makes 6 servings.

Broccoli-Egg Salad

1½ lb. fresh broccoli
4 hard-cooked eggs, chopped
⅓ c. finely chopped onion
⅓ c. chopped pimiento-stuffed
  green olives
1 tblsp. sweet pickle relish
½ c. mayonnaise
¼ tsp. salt
1/16 tsp. pepper

IN ADVANCE:

Cut tough ends from lower stems of broccoli and discard. Peel stems and cut into bite-size pieces. Place in plastic bag and refrigerate.

TO SERVE:

Combine all ingredients in bowl. Toss lightly to mix well. Makes 5 c. or 6 servings.

Buttery Blue Cheese Loaf

⅓ c. butter or regular margarine,
  softened
2 oz. blue cheese, softened
1 tblsp. chives, fresh or freeze-dried
1 (20″) loaf French bread

IN ADVANCE:

Combine butter, cheese and chives in bowl. Beat until well blended using an electric mixer at medium speed. Set aside.

Slice French bread diagonally at ¾″ intervals. Spread slices with butter mixture. Reassemble slices to form a loaf on a 28″ length of heavy-duty foil. Securely wrap loaf into a loose packet and refrigerate.

TO GRILL:

Heat bread on edge of grill 6″ from red coals (high heat), turning once. Grill 15 minutes or until butter mixture is melted and bread is hot. Makes about 6 servings.

SURPRISE SUPPER

Pork Chop Suppers*

Wilted Leaf Lettuce*

Cheesy Whole-wheat Loaf*

Toasted Angel Food Squares*

For each person at your picnic, put a package of Pork Chop Suppers on the grill—then serve up the packets and let everyone discover the individual servings of meat and vegetables in a mushroom gravy. They're delicious served with Cheesy Whole-wheat Loaf, an unusual quick bread with the texture of bran muffins. If your picnic site is just a few steps from the kitchen, add a salad of Wilted Leaf Lettuce with hot bacon dressing. For dessert, let everyone prepare Toasted Angel Food Squares (and have lots of ingredients ready because you're sure to want several!).

Pork Chop Suppers

8 pork chops, ½" thick
½ tsp. salt
⅛ tsp. pepper
8 medium potatoes, pared and cut into
 ¼"-thick slices
8 medium carrots, pared and sliced
8 medium onions, sliced
2 (10¾-oz.) cans condensed golden
 mushroom soup
1 tsp. dried marjoram leaves

Season chops with salt and pepper. Place each pork chop on an 18" length of heavy-duty foil. Arrange potatoes, carrots and onions around each. Spoon mushroom soup over each. Sprinkle with marjoram. Securely wrap each portion into a loose packet.

TO GRILL:

Cook packets 4" from gray coals (medium heat) 50 to 60 minutes or until chops and vegetables are tender. Makes 8 servings.

Wilted Leaf Lettuce

12 strips bacon
½ c. vinegar
¼ c. water
¼ c. sugar
1 tsp. salt
4 qt. torn lettuce leaves (Boston, romaine or garden leaf)
½ c. chopped green onion
4 hard-cooked eggs, chopped

Cook bacon in 12″ skillet over medium heat 6 to 8 minutes or until crisp. Drain on paper towels, crumble and set aside.

Pour off all but 6 tblsp. bacon drippings. Combine drippings with vinegar, water, sugar and salt. Heat to boiling, stirring to dissolve sugar, about 2 minutes.

Combine lettuce, green onion and bacon. Add hot vinegar mixture and toss to coat leaves. Garnish with hard-cooked eggs. Serve at once. Makes 8 servings.

Cheesy Whole-wheat Loaf

2 c. stirred whole-wheat flour
¾ c. sifted flour (all-purpose)
3 tsp. baking powder
1 tsp. baking soda
1½ tsp. salt
2 eggs
1½ c. milk
⅓ c. cooking oil
¼ c. brown sugar, packed
1 tblsp. dried onion flakes
1 c. shredded Swiss cheese

IN ADVANCE:
Stir together whole-wheat flour, all-purpose flour, baking powder, baking soda and salt in mixing bowl.

Combine eggs, milk, oil, brown sugar and onion flakes in another bowl; mix well. Stir in Swiss cheese. Add cheese mixture all at once to dry ingredients, stirring just until moistened. Turn into greased and waxed paper-lined 8½x4½x2½″ loaf pan.

Bake in 375° oven 1 hour or until wooden pick inserted in center comes out clean, covering with foil during the last 15 minutes of baking to prevent overbrowning. Cool in pan on rack 10 minutes. Remove from pan; cool on rack. Makes 1 loaf or about 8 servings.

Toasted Angel Food Squares

1 (9″) angel food cake, cut into 2″ cubes
1 (14-oz.) can sweetened condensed milk
2 (3½-oz.) cans flaked coconut

Dip cake cubes into sweetened condensed milk, then roll in coconut. Press a cake cube onto tines of long-handled fork.

TO GRILL:
Holding fork, grill cake cubes 4″ from gray coals (medium heat), turning often, until coconut is golden brown and cake is warm. Makes 8 servings.

Stuffed Big Burger*

Big Burger Bun*

Make-Your-Own Salad Bar

Amish Oatmeal Cookies*

Praline Ice Cream Sundaes*

Y ou can honor your graduate in a big way with this novel menu. *Stuffed Big Burger* has a melted cheese center spiced with mustard and relish, and is served on a giant sesame seed bun. A flat baking sheet doubles as a giant spatula and makes easy work of turning the super-sized burger. Let the gang serve themselves from a home-style salad bar of mixed greens, raw broccoli flowerets, pickled beets, olives, chopped eggs, bacon bits, croutons and assorted salad dressings. And for dessert, a praline sauce with chopped pecans drizzled over ice cream and served with crunchy oatmeal cookies.

Stuffed Big Burger

2 lb. ground chuck
2 eggs, slightly beaten
2 tblsp. Worcestershire sauce
½ tsp. seasoned salt
¼ tsp. pepper
2 tblsp. prepared mustard
4 slices pasteurized process American
    cheese
¼ c. sweet pickle relish
Big Burger Bun (recipe follows)
toppings: lettuce leaves, sliced tomatoes,
    sliced onion, ketchup

IN ADVANCE:
Combine ground chuck, eggs, Worcestershire sauce, seasoned salt and pepper in bowl. Mix lightly, but well. Divide mixture in half and place each half on a sheet of waxed paper. Shape each half into a 9″ patty.

Spread one patty with mustard; top with cheese and relish. Place second patty on top; pinch patties together to seal well. Cover and refrigerate.

TO GRILL:
Brush top and sides of patty with oil. Grill patty, oiled side down, 4″ from red coals (high heat). Cook 20 to 25 minutes on each side or to desired doneness, brushing with oil once more before turning.

Split Big Burger Bun and place patty on bottom half. Garnish with desired toppings. Add top half of Big Burger Bun. Cut into 8 pie-shaped wedges with a serrated knife. Makes 8 servings.

Big Burger Bun

1 (13¾-oz.) pkg. hot roll mix
¾ c. warm water (105-115°)
1 egg, beaten
1 egg yolk
sesame seeds

Prepare hot roll mix according to package directions, using ¾ c. warm water and egg. Cover; let rise in warm place until doubled, 30 to 45 minutes.

Punch down dough. Turn out on floured surface. Knead until smooth, about 2 minutes. Shape dough into ball. Place on greased baking sheet and flatten to a 9″ circle. Cover; let rise in warm place until almost doubled, 30 to 45 minutes. Beat together egg yolk and 1 tblsp. water. Brush over top of dough and sprinkle with sesame seeds.

Bake in 375° oven 20 minutes or until golden brown. Cool on rack. Makes 1 bun or 8 servings.

Amish Oatmeal Cookies

1½ c. raisins
1 c. salted peanuts
6 c. sifted flour
3 tsp. baking powder
1 tsp. salt
1 tsp. ground cinnamon
1 tsp. ground nutmeg
1½ c. lard or shortening
3 c. sugar
2 c. quick-cooking oats
3 tsp. baking soda
1 c. buttermilk
½ c. molasses
4 eggs

IN ADVANCE:

Grind raisins and peanuts in food grinder, using medium blade; set aside.

Sift together flour, baking powder, salt, cinnamon and nutmeg into very large bowl or dishpan. Cut in lard until mixture forms fine crumbs, using a pastry blender. Add ground raisin mixture, sugar and oats. Mix well, using your hands if necessary.

Dissolve baking soda in buttermilk in small bowl. Add molasses and 3 of the eggs to buttermilk mixture; beat well.

Add buttermilk mixture to flour mixture; mix well with a spoon. Drop mixture by heaping teaspoons or a small ice cream scoop, about 3″ apart, on greased baking sheets. Flatten each with bottom of drinking glass dipped in flour to 2½″ round. Beat remaining egg in small bowl until blended. Brush top of each round with egg.

Bake in 375° oven 8 to 10 minutes or until golden brown. Remove from baking sheets; cool on racks. Makes 4½ doz. cookies.

Praline
Ice Cream Sundaes

½ c. butter or regular margarine
1 c. sifted confectioners' sugar
½ c. water
¼ c. light corn syrup
2 tsp. vanilla
⅔ c. chopped pecans
1½ qt. vanilla ice cream

IN ADVANCE:

Heat butter in 2-qt. saucepan over medium heat until golden brown. Remove from heat and cool.

Gradually add sugar, beating until smooth, using a wooden spoon. Blend in corn syrup and water. Cook over medium heat until sauce boils. Cook, stirring constantly, 1 minute. Remove from heat. Cool 5 minutes. Stir in vanilla and pecans.

Cool slightly before spooning over ice cream; or pour into bowl, cover and refrigerate until ready to serve. Makes 1½ c. or enough sauce for 8 sundaes.

TO REHEAT:

Warm sauce in 1-qt. saucepan over low heat until fluid. Cool slightly before spooning over ice cream.

CHICKEN IN A BASKET

Crispy Fried Chicken*

Confetti Rice Salad*

Parmesan Cheese Crescents*

Elegant Strawberry Torte*

Just about everyone has a favorite fried chicken recipe; this one gives the chicken a crunchy coating flavored with garlic and lemon. Serve it in individual straw baskets with Parmesan Cheese Crescents tucked in alongside the chicken. Confetti Rice Salad is a wonderful-looking side dish with an interesting combination of textures and flavors. For dessert, prepare Elegant Strawberry Torte, a brown-sugary cake topped with golden crumbs and filled with whipped cream and strawberries. The top is circled with soft puffs of whipped cream and more strawberries—dazzling, yet simple.

Crispy Fried Chicken

3 (3-lb.) broiler-fryers, cut up
2 pkg. garlic salad dressing mix
3 tblsp. flour
2 tsp. salt
¼ c. lemon juice
2 tblsp. butter or regular margarine, softened
1 c. milk
1½ c. pancake mix

IN ADVANCE:

Combine salad dressing mix, flour and salt in bowl. Add lemon juice and butter; mix to a smooth paste. Brush chicken on all sides with paste. Stack in bowl; cover and refrigerate overnight.

TO COOK:

About 1½ hours before serving, heat ¼ to ½" oil in large skillet or Dutch oven over medium heat. Dip chicken in milk; then coat well with pancake mix. Shake off excess pancake mix. Lightly brown chicken on all sides in hot oil. As chicken browns, place in shallow baking pan, one layer deep. Spoon half of remaining dipping milk over chicken.

Bake in 375° oven 30 minutes. Remove lid. Baste chicken with remaining dipping milk. Bake 20 to 30 minutes more or until tender. Makes 12 servings.

Confetti Rice Salad

3 c. chicken broth
1½ c. uncooked regular rice
¼ c. salad oil
2 tblsp. cider vinegar
2 tblsp. prepared mustard
1½ tsp. salt
¼ tsp. pepper
1½ c. sliced celery
1 c. sliced ripe olives
½ c. mayonnaise
¼ c. finely chopped onion

¼ c. chopped pimiento
¼ c. pickle relish
2 hard-cooked eggs, diced

IN ADVANCE:
Heat chicken broth in a 2-qt. saucepan over high heat until it comes to a boil. Stir in rice. Reduce heat to low. Cover and cook 20 minutes or until rice is tender.

Combine oil, vinegar, mustard, salt and pepper in a jar. Cover and shake until well blended. Pour over hot rice; toss to mix. Cool well.

Combine cooled rice mixture with remaining ingredients in large bowl. Toss lightly but well. Cover and refrigerate several hours before serving. Makes 12 (¾-c.) servings.

Parmesan Cheese Crescents

2 c. sifted flour
3 tsp. baking powder
1 tsp. salt
½ c. shortening
¾ c. milk
1 tblsp. melted butter or regular margarine
2 tblsp. grated Parmesan cheese
1 tblsp. minced fresh parsley
milk

Sift together flour, baking powder and salt into bowl. Cut in shortening with pastry blender until crumbly. Add ¾ c. milk to flour mixture all at once, stirring just enough with fork to make a soft dough that sticks together.

Turn onto lightly floured surface and knead gently 10 times. Roll into 13″ circle. Brush with melted butter. Sprinkle with Parmesan cheese and parsley. Cut into 12 wedges. Roll up each from wide end. Place crescents, point down, on greased baking sheet. Brush with milk.

Bake in 425° oven 25 minutes or until golden brown. Best served warm. Makes 12 rolls.

Elegant Strawberry Torte

3 c. sifted cake flour
1½ c. brown sugar, packed
½ tsp. salt
1 c. butter or regular margarine
1 egg, beaten
1 c. sour milk
1 tsp. baking soda
½ c. chopped pecans
1 pt. heavy cream, whipped and sweetened
1 pt. fresh strawberries, sliced

IN ADVANCE:
Combine cake flour, brown sugar and salt in bowl. Cut in butter until crumbly, using a pastry blender or two knives. Remove 1 cup of crumb mixture and set aside.

Combine egg, sour milk and baking soda. (To sour milk, place 1 tblsp. vinegar in measuring cup and add enough milk to make 1 c.) Add egg mixture to remaining crumb mixture; blend well. Pour batter into 2 greased and waxed paper-lined 9″ round cake pans. Sprinkle each with reserved 1 c. crumb mixture and pecans.

Bake in 375° oven 25 minutes or until cake tester inserted in center comes out clean. Cool in pans on racks 10 minutes. Remove from pans; cool on racks.

To assemble torte, place one layer on serving plate, crumb side up. Spread with half of the whipped cream. Top with sliced strawberries, reserving 12 slices. Top with second layer, crumb side up. Spoon remaining whipped cream into 12 puffs around the edge of the cake. Top each puff with a strawberry slice.

Chill up to 4 hours (or serve immediately). Makes 12 servings.

Mexican Montage*

Tortilla Chips   Whole-wheat Crackers

Grilled Steak Strips*

Tossed Green Salad

Blue Cheese Dressing*

Vanilla-Walnut Sundaes*

Begin your fiesta with Mexican Montage, a concoction of several south-of-the-border specialties—refried beans, green chilies and taco sauce—built layer upon layer into an interesting appetizer with sour cream, tomatoes, shredded cheese and alfalfa sprouts. While guests are dipping into the appetizer with tortilla chips, thread thin strips of steak on skewers accordian-style and grill. You'll enjoy the party more if you prepare the salad ingredients early in the day (refrigerate right in the salad bowl and cover with a wet paper towel). At the same time, scoop up the ice cream for dessert, stack in a big bowl and freeze until serving time.

Mexican Montage

1 (16-oz.) can refried beans
1 (1⅛-oz.) pkg. taco seasoning mix
⅛ tsp. Tabasco sauce
1 c. dairy sour cream
1 (4-oz.) can green chilies, drained and chopped
½ c. sliced black olives
½ c. shredded Cheddar cheese
½ c. shredded Monterey Jack cheese
½ c. fresh alfalfa sprouts, packed
½ c. chopped tomato
cheese-flavored tortilla chips or crackers
taco sauce

IN ADVANCE:
Combine beans, taco seasoning and Tabasco sauce. Shape mixture into a 6″ circle in the center of a serving plate. Cover and refrigerate. About 1½ hours before serving, remove from refrigerator.

TO SERVE:
Just before serving, spread sour cream over top and sides of bean mixture. Layer in order on top of the sour cream: green chilies, olives, Cheddar cheese, Monterey Jack cheese, alfalfa sprouts and chopped tomato. Serve with tortilla chips or crackers and taco sauce. Makes 10 servings.

Grilled Steak Strips

3 lb. boneless beef sirloin steak, 1" thick
1½ c. soy sauce
1½ c. water
1⅓ c. sugar
2 green onions, finely chopped
4 cloves garlic, minced
¼ tsp. ground ginger

IN ADVANCE:

Freeze steak until partially frozen. Cut steak crosswise into 3x⅛" strips. Set aside.

Combine remaining ingredients in bowl, stirring until sugar dissolves. Add steak, cover and refrigerate 24 hours, stirring 2 or 3 times while marinating.

TO GRILL:

Thread steak strips on 6 skewers. Grill kabobs 4" from gray coals (medium heat), turning and basting with marinade every 5 minutes. Cook 15 minutes or to desired doneness. Makes 10 servings.

Blue Cheese Dressing

1½ c. mayonnaise
1 c. dairy sour cream
4 oz. blue cheese, crumbled
¼ c. finely chopped onion
2 tblsp. cider vinegar
2 tblsp. lemon juice
1 small clove garlic, minced
½ tsp. sugar
⅛ tsp. pepper

IN ADVANCE:

Combine all ingredients in bowl. Mix well. Cover and refrigerate at least 3 hours before serving. Makes 3 c.

Vanilla-Walnut Sundaes

1½ c. brown sugar, packed
½ c. light corn syrup
¼ c. butter or regular margarine
⅛ tsp. salt
½ c. heavy cream
1 tsp. vanilla
1½ c. broken walnuts
1½ qt. vanilla ice cream

IN ADVANCE:

Combine brown sugar, corn syrup, butter and salt in 2-qt. saucepan. Cook over medium heat until mixture comes to a boil. Cook 3 minutes more. Remove from heat and cool 5 minutes. Add cream and vanilla and mix until well blended. Stir in walnuts.

Serve sauce warm over ice cream; or pour into a bowl, cover and refrigerate until ready to serve. Makes 10 servings.

TO REHEAT:

Pour sauce into 2-qt. saucepan and warm over medium heat.

Chunky Chicken Salad on Rye*

Frozen Cuke and Onion Relish*

Marathon Cookies*

Watermelon Wedges

Fruit Cooler*

When someone says, "What a beautiful day for a picnic!" you can say "Let's go!"—if you've stocked your freezer for spur-of-the-moment excursions. Keep lots of cooked, cubed chicken in the freezer for quick sandwich makings, and freeze batches of homemade concentrate for a refreshing Fruit Cooler. Frozen Cuke and Onion Relish and the high-energy Marathon Cookies can be packed straight from the freezer—there's no need to thaw. Tuck in a few hard-cooked eggs, and you're ready to go.

Chunky Chicken Salad on Rye

4 c. cooked, cubed chicken (¾" cubes)
1 c. chopped celery
½ c. chopped onion
⅓ c. chopped fresh parsley
1 c. mayonnaise
¼ c. salad oil
2 tblsp. lemon juice
¼ tsp. sugar
¼ tsp. salt
⅛ tsp. pepper
16 slices pasteurized process
   American cheese
16 slices rye or pumpernickel bread
4 medium tomatoes, sliced
16 lettuce leaves

IN ADVANCE:
  Combine chicken, celery, onion, parsley, mayonnaise, oil, lemon juice, sugar, salt and pepper in bowl. Toss lightly to mix well. Cover and refrigerate.
TO SERVE:
  Place 2 slices of cheese on each of 8 slices bread. Top each with 3 slices tomato, about ½ c. chicken salad and 2 lettuce leaves. Top each with a slice of bread. Makes 8 sandwiches.

Marinated Beef Kabobs (p. 80).

Clockwise from top: Sour Cream Potato Salad (p. 90), Kidney Bean Salad (p. 116), and Tangy Coleslaw (p. 55).

From top: Bacon-Onion Sticks, Summer
Sparkle Punch, Blueberry Cake Squares,
and Hot Frank Potato Salad (pp. 50-51).

Clockwise from upper right: Pears in
Mint Sauce (p. 15), Orange Sherbet Molds
(p. 71) and Fresh Fruit Compote (p. 99).

Frozen Cuke and Onion Relish

4 qt. (8 large) sliced cucumbers
4 c. sliced onion
1⅓ c. sugar
1⅓ c. vinegar
3 tblsp. salt

IN ADVANCE:

Combine all ingredients in bowl. Toss lightly to mix well. Set aside for 10 minutes. Divide equally into 4 (1-qt.) freezer-proof containers. Cover and freeze until ready to serve.

Thaw slightly before serving. Makes 4 qt. or 8 to 10 servings.

Marathon Cookies

1½ c. cut-up dried apricots
2 c. water
2 c. sifted flour
1 tsp. baking soda
1 tsp. ground cinnamon
½ tsp. salt
¾ c. butter or regular margarine
½ c. peanut butter
2 c. brown sugar, packed
2 eggs
¼ c. milk
1 tsp. vanilla
1½ c. natural granola cereal
1 c. raisins
1 c. peanuts

IN ADVANCE:

Combine apricots and water in a 2-qt. saucepan. Cook over high heat until mixture comes to a boil. Reduce heat to medium and cook 5 minutes or until apricots are tender. Drain; cool completely.

Meanwhile, sift together flour, baking soda, cinnamon and salt; set aside.

Cream together butter, peanut butter and brown sugar in mixing bowl until light and fluffy, using an electric mixer at medium speed. Add eggs, one at a time, beating well after each addition. Blend in milk and vanilla.

Gradually stir dry ingredients into creamed mixture, blending well. Stir in granola cereal, raisins, peanuts and apricots. Drop mixture by heaping tablespoonfuls, about 3" apart, on greased baking sheets.

Bake in 350° oven 18 to 20 minutes or until golden brown. Remove from baking sheets; cool on racks. Makes about 3½ doz. cookies.

TO FREEZE:

Wrap in aluminum foil or plastic wrap.

Fruit Cooler

1 (20-oz.) can sliced or chunk pineapple in juice
2¼ c. fresh lemon juice
1 c. fresh orange juice
1 c. cranberry juice
1½ c. sugar
9 c. water

IN ADVANCE:

Purée undrained pineapple in blender or food processor at high speed; pour into bowl. Stir in lemon juice, orange juice, cranberry juice and sugar. Mix well.

Pour about 1⅔ c. of the concentrate mixture into each of three plastic bowls or freezer-proof containers. Cover and freeze.

TO SERVE:

Thaw frozen concentrate. Add 3 c. water to each portion, stirring until blended. Chill or serve over ice. Makes about 1 gal. or 16 (8-oz.) servings.

Chilled Cranberry Soup*

Sausage-stuffed Turkey on a Spit*

Garden-fresh Asparagus

Cucumbers in Sour Cream*

Ice Creamwiches*

Celebrate our heritage of good country cooking with these updated versions of traditional American recipes. Whole cranberries in a ruby-red sauce flavored with cinnamon and cloves are the makings of Chilled Cranberry Soup. Sausage-stuffed Turkey on a Spit cooks over the grill in the same amount of time as an oven-roasted bird. A side dish of Cucumbers in Sour Cream provides a cool accompaniment. For dessert, Ice Cream-wiches—homemade ice cream sandwiches—offer a wonderful contrast of flavor and texture.

Chilled Cranberry Soup

3 c. water
1½ c. sugar
2 cinnamon sticks
¼ tsp. ground cloves
4 c. cranberries
2 tblsp. lemon juice
1 tblsp. grated orange rind
sour cream
2 oranges, thinly sliced
ground cinnamon

IN ADVANCE:

Combine water, sugar, cinnamon sticks and ground cloves in 4-qt. Dutch oven. Cook over high heat until mixture comes to a boil, about 10 minutes. Add cranberries and cook until mixture returns to a boil. Reduce heat to medium. Cook 5 minutes or until cranberry skins begin to pop.

Remove from heat. Stir in lemon juice and orange rind. Set aside to cool for about 45 minutes. Remove cinnamon sticks. Cover and refrigerate at least 4 hours.

TO SERVE:

Top each serving with a dollop of sour cream, orange slice twist and a sprinkle of cinnamon. Makes 5 c. or 10 (½-c.) servings.

Sausage-stuffed Turkey on a Spit

1 lb. bulk pork sausage
¾ c. chopped onion
¾ c. chopped celery
4 c. fresh bread cubes (½" cubes)
1 c. chicken broth
¼ c. chopped fresh parsley
1 tsp. rubbed sage leaves
1 tsp. poultry seasoning
1 (8-lb.) turkey

IN ADVANCE:

Cook sausage, onion and celery in 10" skillet over medium heat until meat is browned and vegetables are tender. Remove from heat. Add bread cubes, chicken broth, parsley, sage and poultry seasoning. Toss lightly to mix well. Place mixture in bowl. Cover and refrigerate.

TO GRILL:

Loosely stuff cavity of turkey with stuffing mixture. Close cavity and secure with skewers. Truss. Run spit through center of turkey. Set spit forks in breast and thigh and tighten. Holding spit at both ends, turn. If one side of turkey drops downward, reposition turkey so it is balanced. Securely tie wings and legs to body.

Place on grill rotisserie, close lid and grill over light gray coals (low heat). Cook 3 to 3½ hours until meat thermometer inserted in stuffing registers 165°. Makes 10 to 14 servings.

Cucumbers in Sour Cream

8 c. sliced, pared cucumbers
½ c. thinly sliced onion
4 tsp. salt
2 c. dairy sour cream
1 tblsp. chopped fresh dill
1 tsp. cider vinegar
4 drops Tabasco sauce

IN ADVANCE:

Combine cucumbers, onion and salt in bowl. Toss lightly to mix well. Cover and set aside for 30 minutes. Drain well.

Add sour cream, dill, vinegar and Tabasco sauce to drained cucumbers. Toss lightly to mix well. Cover and refrigerate at least 2 hours before serving. Makes 10 servings.

Ice Creamwiches

1 qt. vanilla or chocolate ice cream
20 (2½") round oatmeal cookies

IN ADVANCE:

Place 1 scoop ice cream on each of 10 cookies. Top each cookie with another cookie. Press together tightly. Wrap in plastic wrap and store in freezer. Makes 10 servings.

Teriyaki Flank Steak*

Golden Rice Pilaf*

Easy Spinach Soufflé*

Super Cyder Floats*

I f you live in a small community where Memorial Day is marked by a parade—complete with processions of Scout troops, baton-twirlers and the local high school's marching band— you're very likely to join in a picnic after all the hoopla is over. Teriyaki Flank Steak is easier and much less messy than the classic variety because it cooks directly on the grill without having to be threaded onto skewers— yet it has the same wonderful flavor. Serve it with Golden Rice Pilaf and Easy Spinach Soufflé, and finish the meal with a flourish by passing frosty mugs of vanilla ice cream and apple cider.

Teriyaki Flank Steak

¾ c. cooking oil
¼ c. soy sauce
3 tblsp. honey
2 tblsp. wine vinegar
1½ tsp. ground ginger
1 green onion, finely chopped
2 cloves garlic, minced
2 to 2½ lb. flank steak or London broil, 1" thick

IN ADVANCE:
   Combine cooking oil, soy sauce, honey, vinegar, ginger, onion and garlic in 12x8x2" (2-qt.) baking dish. Mix well. Set aside. Score steak on both sides. Add steak to marinade, turning to coat both sides. Cover and refrigerate over-night, turning occasionally.
TO GRILL:
   Cook steak 6" from red-gray coals (high heat). Grill 10 to 12 minutes on each side or to desired doneness, basting often with marinade. To serve, cut diagonally into very thin slices. Makes 6 to 8 servings.

Golden Rice Pilaf

½ c. butter or regular margarine
1 c. chopped onion
1 c. shredded, pared carrots
½ c. sliced celery
½ c. chopped green pepper
2 cloves garlic, minced
1½ c. uncooked regular rice
1¾ c. chicken broth
1 c. water
¼ c. chopped fresh parsley
½ tsp. salt
⅛ tsp. pepper

Melt 2 tblsp. of the butter in 12″ electric frypan preheated to 300°. Sauté onion, carrots, celery, green pepper and garlic in butter until tender. Remove vegetables from frypan and set aside.

Melt remaining 6 tblsp. butter in same frypan. Add rice and cook, stirring constantly, until rice is browned and most of the butter has been absorbed, about 10 minutes. Stir in chicken broth, water, parsley, salt, pepper and sautéed vegetables. Increase temperature to 400°. Cook until mixture comes to a boil. Reduce temperature to 220°.

Cover and simmer 20 minutes or until rice is tender. Fluff with fork before serving. Makes 8 servings.

Easy Spinach Soufflé

2 c. creamed cottage cheese
½ c. shredded Cheddar cheese
3 eggs
⅓ c. flour
¼ c. melted butter or regular margarine
¾ tsp. salt
¼ tsp. ground nutmeg
⅛ tsp. pepper
2 (10-oz.) pkg. frozen chopped spinach, thawed and drained

Place cottage cheese, Cheddar cheese, eggs, flour, butter, salt, nutmeg and pepper in a blender. Cover and blend at high speed for 1 minute. Mix with spinach. Turn into greased 2-qt. soufflé dish. Set dish in a pan of hot water.

Bake in 350° oven 1 hour or until mixture is set. Makes 8 servings.

Super Cyder Floats

2 qt. apple cider, chilled
1 qt. vanilla ice cream
ground nutmeg

Pour 1 c. cider into 8 old-fashioned root beer mugs or tall glasses. Top each with a scoop of ice cream. Sprinkle with nutmeg. Makes 8 (12-oz.) floats.

Summer Reunions

Whether you're organizing a reunion of four generations of family or planning an impromptu supper for a few good friends, everyone's mood will be more relaxed if you move the meal outdoors.

The menus in this chapter are designed to keep cooking to a minimum and to make maximum use of the grill. Three menus in this chapter can be cooked entirely on the grill, including the dessert: Campers' Choice (p. 72), A Complete Meal on the Grill (p. 92), and Lazy Day Barbecue (p. 96). Many other menus feature meat-and-vegetable combinations that can be roasted over the coals while you enjoy the company and the conversation.

Our mainland-based Hawaiian Luau (p. 64), starts with bacon-wrapped chicken livers and teams colorful vegetable kabobs with a Tennessee farm woman's recipe for spareribs glazed with a peachy sweet-sour sauce. For Father's Day—or any other day you'd like to treat someone to a robust outdoor meal—there are recipes for Mixed Grill and a Ratatouille made with garden-fresh eggplant, zucchini, tomatoes and onions (p. 58).

But you don't have to live in the country to enjoy outdoor meals—some of these menus were designed for metropolitan areas. Olive-stuffed Meatballs and Eggplant au Gratin make up the City-style Cookout (p. 52) that you can grill at the edge of a lake or anywhere you can set up a hibachi. Or plan a Block Party Barbecue (p. 70) featuring tender, crispy ribs glazed with a sweet-sour sauce, and a colorful macaroni salad flavored with shredded cheese and hard-cooked eggs.

Main-dish salads are a good way to beat the heat; Layered Salmon Salad is a light, elegant entrée that forms the basis of our Midsummer Night's Supper (p. 74). For a main-dish salad with a little more spice, there's a Wisconsin woman's recipe for Taco Salad that blends ground beef, tomatoes, Cheddar cheese, crunchy tortilla chips and sour cream (p. 88).

Any of these recipes can easily be doubled or tripled to serve a large group, but you can serve 20 with every recipe in our Family Reunion menu (p. 54)—it includes classic deviled eggs, barbecued chicken, coleslaw and a bubbly fruit-flavored punch. Another big-batch menu is the Community Cookout (p. 86), with recipes for a dozen servings of barbecued chicken wings as appetizers, grilled Pork with a Peppery Peanut Dip, hot rolls with a pizza-flavored filling and a big bowl of frosty Lime Slush Punch.

Cold beverages are a must during the sultry summer months, so we've included recipes for a dozen punches, fizzes and floats, including a Melonade Cooler made from fresh watermelon (p. 61), a Strawberry-Pineapple Flip (p. 47), a Tangerine-Apple Nectar (p. 85), Raspberry-Lemon Fizz (p. 54), and a recipe for a homemade fruity sangria (p. 89).

In this chapter you'll find more than enough menus and recipes for every week of summer—together with ideas for enjoying the season to the fullest.

Chicken with Sweet Potatoes*

Dilly Cucumber Mold*

Swiss Rye Loaf*

Strawberry-Pineapple Flip*

T*his simple but elegant menu was planned with casual preparation in mind, leaving you free to enjoy the fresh air. Individual packets of chicken and sweet potatoes simmer over the coals in a flavorful prepared gravy until moist and tender. Pass a basket of hot Swiss Rye Loaf—each warm and buttery slice has a hint of mustard and lots of melted Swiss cheese. When lunch is ready to be served, unmold the cool cucumber salad and offer frosty glasses of Strawberry-Pineapple Flip.*

Chicken with Sweet Potatoes

*6 chicken thighs
6 chicken drumsticks
6 fresh sweet potatoes or yams, pared and sliced
6 small onions, sliced
salt
pepper
2 (10½-oz.) cans chicken gravy*

IN ADVANCE:

Arrange 1 chicken thigh, 1 chicken drumstick and an equal amount of potato and onion on each of 6 (18") lengths of heavy-duty foil. Sprinkle with salt and pepper. Pour an equal amount of chicken gravy over each. Securely wrap each portion into a loose packet and refrigerate.

TO GRILL:

Cook chicken-vegetable packets 4" from gray coals (medium heat) on a covered grill with lid closed. Grill 45 minutes or until chicken is tender. Makes 6 servings.

Dilly Cucumber Mold

1 (3-oz.) pkg. lime-flavored gelatin
1 c. boiling water
2 tblsp. lemon juice
1½ c. finely chopped, pared cucumber
1 c. dairy sour cream
½ c. finely chopped celery
2 tblsp. minced green onion
½ tsp. dried dill
cucumber slices

IN ADVANCE:

Combine lime gelatin and boiling water in bowl, stirring until gelatin is completely dissolved. Stir in lemon juice. Refrigerate 45 to 60 minutes or until thickened.

Fold in cucumber, sour cream, celery, onion and dill. Pour into 4-c. mold. Refrigerate 2 to 2½ hours or until set.

TO SERVE:

Unmold gelatin and garnish with cucumber slices. Makes 6 servings.

Swiss Rye Loaf

1 c. shredded Swiss cheese
½ c. butter or regular margarine, softened
1 tblsp. Dijon mustard
1 (1-lb.) loaf sliced rye bread

IN ADVANCE:

Combine cheese, butter and mustard in bowl. Beat until well blended, using an electric mixer at medium speed. Spread one side of each slice of bread with cheese mixture. Reassemble slices in loaf form on 18" length of heavy-duty foil. Securely wrap loaf into a tight packet and refrigerate.

TO GRILL:

Heat bread 4" from gray coals (medium heat), turning occasionally.

Grill about 30 minutes or until butter mixture is melted and bread is hot. Makes 1 loaf.

Strawberry-Pineapple Flip

1 (10-oz.) pkg. frozen strawberries, thawed
3 c. pineapple juice
2 (12-oz.) cans lemon-lime soda, chilled

IN ADVANCE:

Purée strawberries with their own juice in blender. Combine puréed strawberries and pineapple juice. Cover and refrigerate.

TO SERVE:

Stir lemon-lime soda into strawberry-pineapple juice. Serve over ice in glasses. Makes 7 c. or 6 servings.

Curried Squash Bisque*

Marinated Pork Kabobs*

Whole-wheat Pita*

Peach Ice Cream Sundaes*

For a carefree summertime supper, serve soup and sandwiches right in your own backyard. Curried Squash Bisque is a smooth, golden blend of fresh yellow summer squash and carrots with a cheesy base. Marinated Pork Kabobs are served in homemade pita bread with a fresh Cucumber-Yogurt Sauce. The hot pork and cool sauce treat your taste buds to a wonderful contrast of flavors. For dessert, scoop up ice cream sundaes topped with a fresh peach sauce.

Curried Squash Bisque

1 c. sliced, pared carrots
½ c. chopped onion
¾ tsp. salt
1 chicken bouillon cube
1 c. water
2 medium yellow summer squash
¼ c. flour
2 c. milk
1 tsp. curry powder
1 c. shredded Cheddar cheese
1 (13-oz.) can evaporated milk

IN ADVANCE:
Combine carrots, onion, salt, bouillon cube and water in a 3-qt. saucepan. Cook over high heat until mixture comes to a boil. Reduce heat to low. Cover and simmer 5 minutes.

Cut squash in half lengthwise and cut into ¼" slices. Add to simmering mixture. Cover and simmer 5 minutes more, or until vegetables are tender.

Meanwhile, combine flour and milk in jar. Cover and shake until blended and smooth. Stir flour mixture and curry powder into vegetable mixture. Cook over medium heat, stirring constantly, until mixture thickens.

Remove from heat. Slowly add cheese and evaporated milk, stirring until cheese melts. Pour into bowl; cover and refrigerate.

TO REHEAT:
Warm over medium heat until hot. Makes 1½ qt. or 6 servings.

Marinated Pork Kabobs

2 lb. boneless lean pork, cut into 1" cubes
½ c. cooking oil
3 tblsp. lemon juice
¼ c. finely chopped onion
1 tblsp. minced fresh parsley
1 clove garlic, minced
¾ tsp. salt

⅛ tsp. pepper
½ tsp. dried marjoram leaves
Cucumber-Yogurt Sauce (recipe follows)
6 Whole-wheat Pita (recipe follows)

IN ADVANCE:

Combine pork, oil, lemon juice, onion, parsley, garlic, salt, pepper and marjoram in glass bowl. Cover and refrigerate overnight.

TO GRILL:

Thread pork cubes on 6 (12″) skewers. Grill kabobs 4″ from gray coals (medium heat), turning often and basting with marinade. Cook 15 minutes or until no longer pink in center. Prepare Cucumber-Yogurt Sauce. To serve, stuff Whole-wheat Pita with pork and top with Cucumber-Yogurt Sauce. Makes 6 sandwiches.

CUCUMBER-YOGURT SAUCE: Combine 1 (8-oz.) container plain yogurt, ½ c. chopped cucumber, 1 tblsp. minced onion, 1 tblsp. minced fresh parsley, 1 tsp. lemon juice and ⅛ tsp. garlic salt in bowl; mix well.

Whole-wheat Pita

4 c. stirred whole-wheat flour
2 tblsp. brown sugar, packed
2 pkg. active dry yeast
2 tsp. salt
¼ c. shortening
2½ c. very warm water (120° to 130°)
1 to 1½ c. sifted flour (all-purpose)
yellow corn meal

IN ADVANCE:

Combine 3 c. of the whole-wheat flour, brown sugar, yeast and salt in a bowl. Mix well.

Add shortening and very warm water. Beat until smooth, using an electric mixer at medium speed. Stir in remaining 1 c. whole-wheat flour and enough all-purpose flour to make a soft dough.

Turn dough out onto lightly floured surface. Knead until smooth, about 10 minutes. Place in greased bowl, turning over once to grease top. Cover; let rise until doubled, about 30 minutes.

Punch down dough; divide into 12 pieces. Shape each into a ball and place on greased baking sheets. Cover; let rise 30 minutes.

Sprinkle 4 greased baking sheets with corn meal. Roll out each ball to 6″ circle, and place 3 circles of dough on each baking sheet. Cover; let rise 30 minutes.

Bake in 475° oven 8 to 10 minutes or until lightly browned. Cool completely and wrap in foil.) Makes 12 pitas.

TO REHEAT:

Warm foil-wrapped pitas on grill.

Peach Ice Cream Sundaes

4 c. sliced, pared peaches
¾ c. brown sugar, packed
¾ c. orange juice
⅛ tsp. ground nutmeg
2 tsp. grated orange rind
1 tsp. vanilla
1½ qt. vanilla ice cream
½ c. toasted slivered almonds
6 maraschino cherries

IN ADVANCE:

Combine peaches, brown sugar, orange juice and nutmeg in a 2-qt. saucepan. Cook over high heat until mixture comes to a boil. Reduce heat to low and simmer 15 minutes or until peaches are tender. Remove from heat. Stir in orange rind and vanilla.

Refrigerate in covered bowl.

TO SERVE:

Scoop ice cream into 6 sundae glasses. Spoon about ½ c. peach sauce over each. Top with almonds and a maraschino cherry. Makes 6 sundaes.

Hot Frank Potato Salad*

Bacon-Onion Sticks*

Blueberry Cake Squares*

Summer Sparkle Punch*

This moveable feast can be toted to a faraway farm home, a town park, or your own back porch. The menu features the kinds of dishes where the pans are always empty when you go home and everyone asks for the recipes. The main-dish potato salad is meant to be served warm and it has sliced frankfurters mixed right in with the potatoes. Bacon-Onion Sticks are an "old-country" favorite that originated in Latvia; the recipe has been handed down through generations of one farm family. The blueberry cake is a light, moist cake with plump blueberries swirled into the batter—all it needs is a dusting of confectioners' sugar. Summer Sparkle Punch has just the right amount of sweetness and fresh fruit flavor.

Hot Frank Potato Salad

6 c. sliced, cooked potatoes
8 frankfurters, sliced
2 hard-cooked eggs, chopped
½ lb. bacon strips
¾ c. chopped onion
3 tblsp. sugar
3 tblsp. flour
1½ tsp. salt
1 tsp. celery seed
¾ c. cider vinegar
1½ c. water
chopped fresh parsley

IN ADVANCE:
Combine potatoes, frankfurters and eggs in bowl. Toss lightly to mix well. Set aside.

Fry bacon in 10" skillet over medium heat 5 minutes or until crisp. Remove bacon with slotted spoon; drain on paper towels and crumble.

Pour off all but ⅓ c. bacon drippings. Sauté onion in remaining drippings until tender. Blend in sugar, flour, salt and celery seed. Stir in vinegar and water. Cook, stirring constantly, until mixture boils and thickens.

Pour over potato mixture. Add bacon. Toss together lightly to mix well. Turn into a greased 3-qt casserole. Cover and refrigerate.

TO COOK:
Bake in 350° oven 50 minutes or until hot and bubbly. Garnish with chopped parsley. Makes 8 servings.

Bacon-Onion Sticks

2 pkg. active dry yeast
2 c. lukewarm milk (110°)
1 tsp. salt
1 tsp. sugar
½ c. butter or regular margarine, melted
1 tsp. ground cardamom
5½ to 6 c. sifted flour
1 lb. bacon, diced
1¼ c. chopped onion

¼ tsp. salt
¼ tsp. pepper
1 egg, beaten
salt crystals

IN ADVANCE:

Combine yeast and milk in large bowl. Stir until yeast is dissolved.

Add 1 tsp. salt, sugar, butter, cardamom and 2½ c. of the flour to milk mixture. Beat until smooth, about 2 minutes, using an electric mixer at medium speed.

Gradually stir in enough remaining flour to make a soft dough. Turn dough out onto floured surface and knead until smooth and satiny, about 8 to 10 minutes.

Place dough in greased bowl, turning over once to grease top. Cover and let rise in warm place until doubled, about 1 hour and 15 minutes.

Meanwhile, sauté bacon and onion in 12″ skillet over medium heat until bacon is browned and onion is tender. Drain on paper towels. Add ¼ tsp. salt and pepper and toss lightly to mix well. Cool completely.

Turn dough out onto floured surface and knead bacon mixture into dough. Roll dough into a 14″ square. Brush dough with egg and sprinkle with salt crystals. Cut dough in half lengthwise and into thirds crosswise. Cut each section into 6 sticks. Place on greased baking sheet and let rise until doubled, about 30 to 45 minutes.

Bake in 375° oven 15 minutes or until golden brown. Makes 36 sticks.

Blueberry Cake Squares

3 c. sifted flour
2 tsp. baking powder
½ tsp. salt
1 c. shortening
1½ c. sugar
4 eggs, separated
2 tsp. vanilla

⅔ c. milk
½ c. sugar
3 c. fresh blueberries
1 tblsp. flour
confectioners' sugar

IN ADVANCE:

Sift together flour, baking powder and salt; set aside.

Cream together shortening and 1½ c. sugar in bowl until light and fluffy, using an electric mixer at medium speed. Add egg yolks and vanilla; beat until light and fluffy.

Add dry ingredients alternately with milk to creamed mixture, beating well after each addition. Set aside.

Beat egg whites in bowl until foamy, using an electric mixer at high speed. Gradually add ½ c. sugar, 1 tblsp. at a time, beating until stiff peaks form. Gradually fold into batter. Mix blueberries with 1 tblsp. flour and stir into batter. Pour batter into a greased 13x9x2″ baking pan.

Bake in 350° oven 50 minutes or until cake tester or wooden pick inserted in center comes out clean. Cool in pan on rack. Sprinkle with sifted confectioners' sugar. Makes 12 servings.

Summer Sparkle Punch

2 (3-oz.) pkg. strawberry-flavored gelatin
2 c. boiling water
2 (12-oz.) cans frozen lemonade concentrate, slightly thawed
3 (28-oz.) bottles ginger ale, chilled
ice cubes

IN ADVANCE:

Combine gelatin and boiling water in bowl, stirring until gelatin is completely dissolved. Stir in lemonade. Cover and refrigerate until ready to serve.

TO SERVE:

Add ginger ale and ice cubes to chilled mixture. Stir well. Makes 1 gal. or 8 servings.

CITY-STYLE COOKOUT

Olive-stuffed Meatballs*

Eggplant au Gratin*

Tomato-Onion Salad*

Chilled Peach Squares*

City dwellers can picnic and barbecue without having to forsake the city; almost any nice spot can be a picnic site—even a high-rise apartment balcony. You'll feel as if you're in the country almost as soon as you step outdoors. Eggplant au Gratin is an easy-to-prepare vegetable dish of sliced eggplant dipped in cheese-flavored crumbs and topped with triangles of mozzarella cheese. While the eggplant cooks, prepare Olive-stuffed Meatballs. The olives add a flavorful surprise and make it easy to skewer the meatballs. Serve a simple grill-side salad and a dessert of Chilled Peach Squares, a picnic favorite from a Pennsylvania farm family.

Olive-stuffed Meatballs

1½ lb. ground beef
½ c. quick-cooking oats
¼ c. milk
1 egg
1 tsp. Worcestershire sauce
½ tsp. salt
¼ tsp. dry mustard
18 pimiento-stuffed olives
barbecue sauce

IN ADVANCE:
Combine ground beef, oats, milk, egg, Worcestershire sauce, salt and dry mustard in bowl. Mix lightly, but well. Form mixture into 18 meatballs, shaping each around an olive.
Thread meatballs on 6 (12″) skewers. Place on baking sheet or in baking pan. Cover and refrigerate.
TO GRILL:
Brush kabobs with your favorite barbecue sauce. Grill kabobs 4″ from gray coals (medium heat), gently turning and basting often with sauce. Cook 30 minutes or to desired doneness. Makes 6 servings.

Eggplant au Gratin

2 lb. eggplant
salt
pepper
⅔ c. butter or regular margarine, melted
⅔ c. finely crushed cheese crackers
1 (8-oz.) pkg. mozzarella cheese slices, cut diagonally in half

IN ADVANCE:
Peel eggplant and cut into 12 slices. Sprinkle each slice with salt and pepper. Dip each slice in butter and then in cracker crumbs. Place 2 slices of eggplant on an 18″ length of heavy-duty

foil. Securely wrap into a loose packet and refrigerate.

TO GRILL:

Cook eggplant packets 4″ from gray coals (medium heat), turning once. Cook 30 to 40 minutes or until tender.

Open each packet and top each eggplant slice with one cheese triangle. Cook 2 to 3 minutes longer or until cheese is melted. Makes 6 servings.

Tomato-Onion Salad

6 medium tomatoes (about 2 lb.)
1 c. sliced onion
¾ c. salad oil
¼ c. vinegar
½ tsp. dry mustard
½ tsp. paprika
½ tsp. salt
⅛ tsp. pepper
1 c. dairy sour cream
1 tblsp. chopped fresh parsley

IN ADVANCE:

Peel tomatoes and slice. Layer tomatoes and onion in bowl. Combine oil, vinegar, mustard, paprika, salt and pepper in jar. Cover and shake until blended. Pour dressing over tomatoes and onion. Cover and refrigerate.

TO SERVE:

Combine sour cream and parsley in bowl; mix well. Top each serving of salad with a dollop of sour cream dressing. Makes 6 servings.

Chilled Peach Squares

1½ c. graham cracker crumbs
¼ c. butter or regular margarine, melted
4 c. sliced, pared peaches
½ c. sifted confectioners' sugar
water
1 (3-oz.) pkg. orange-flavored gelatin
1 c. boiling water
1 c. heavy cream, whipped

IN ADVANCE:

Combine cracker crumbs and butter in bowl. Mix well and press half of mixture into each of two 8″ square baking pans. Refrigerate while preparing the filling.

Combine peaches and confectioners' sugar in large bowl and let stand 30 minutes.

Drain peaches, reserving juice. Add enough water to juice to make 1 c.; set aside with peaches. Combine gelatin and boiling water in bowl, stirring until gelatin is completely dissolved. Stir in reserved peach juice.

Refrigerate 45 to 60 minutes or until partially set.

Fold in whipped cream and peaches. Pour half of peach-cream mixture into each prepared crumb crust pan.

Refrigerate several hours or until well chilled. Makes 12 servings.

Deviled Party Eggs*

Big-Batch Chicken Barbecue*

Tangy Coleslaw*

Baking Powder Biscuits

Fruit-and-Cheese Platter

Sparkling Citrus Punch*

Whether your family numbers 20 or 200, this menu works well because each recipe can be doubled and redoubled to serve as many as needed. Big-Batch Chicken Barbecue has a delicious piquant flavor and a lightly crisped skin. Pair it with Tangy Coleslaw, and cooking for a crowd needn't be a chore. Pack the garnish for the deviled eggs separately to add the finishing touch when you reach your destination. If you're picnicking near home, mix up a big bowl of Sparkling Citrus Punch, a flavorful combination of five fruit juices.

Deviled Party Eggs

12 hard-cooked eggs
½ c. mayonnaise
2 tblsp. chopped chives, fresh or dried
4 tsp. prepared yellow mustard
¼ tsp. salt
garnishes: sliced olives, pimiento strips, chopped fresh parsley, small canned shrimp or bacon bits

IN ADVANCE:

Peel eggs and cut in half lengthwise. Remove yolks and place in bowl. Break up yolks until fine and crumbly, using an electric mixer at low speed. Add mayonnaise, chives, mustard and salt; beat until smooth.

Pipe yolk mixture into egg whites, using a pastry bag with a large (#4) star tip or spoon into egg whites, using a teaspoon. Garnish as you wish.

Cover and refrigerate up to 6 hours before serving. Makes 24.

Big-Batch Chicken Barbecue

5 broiler-fryers, quartered
1 c. cider vinegar
½ c. cooking oil
1 egg
2¼ tsp. salt
1½ tsp. poultry seasoning
¼ tsp. pepper

IN ADVANCE:

Arrange chicken in large roasting pan. Combine vinegar, oil, egg, salt, poultry seasoning and pepper in bowl. Mix well. Pour marinade over chicken. Cover and refrigerate overnight, turning occasionally.

Cook chicken 4″ from gray coals (medium heat), turning and basting with marinade every 10 minutes. Cook 1 hour or until tender. Makes 20 servings.

Tangy Coleslaw

2 c. cider vinegar
2 c. sugar
1½ tsp. mustard seeds
1½ tsp. celery seeds
1 tsp. salt
½ tsp. ground turmeric
20 c. shredded cabbage
3 c. chopped onion
2 (4-oz.) jars pimientos, drained
  and chopped

IN ADVANCE:
Combine vinegar, sugar, mustard seeds, celery seeds, salt and turmeric in a 2-qt. saucepan. Cook over medium heat, stirring occasionally, until mixture boils. Remove from heat and cool to room temperature.

Combine cabbage, onion and pimientos in a very large bowl. Pour vinegar mixture over cabbage mixture. Toss lightly to mix well.

Cover and refrigerate overnight. Makes 20 servings.

Sparkling Citrus Punch

3 lemons, sliced
3 limes, sliced
1 (6-oz.) can frozen orange juice
  concentrate
1 (6-oz.) can frozen grapefruit juice
  concentrate
1 (6-oz.) can frozen tangerine juice
  concentrate
1 (6-oz.) can frozen lemonade concentrate
½ c. lime juice, fresh or bottled
6 c. water
2 (28-oz.) bottles club soda, chilled

IN ADVANCE:
Pour 1 c. water into 6-cup ring mold. Freeze. Alternately arrange lemon and lime slices on top of ice ring, overlapping edges. Add just enough water to cover fruit. Freeze until ready to prepare punch.

TO SERVE:
Combine concentrates of orange juice, grapefruit juice, tangerine juice and lemonade in punch bowl with lime juice, 6 c. water and club soda. Mix well.

Unmold ice ring by dipping the mold into hot water. Float ice ring in punch. Makes about 1 gal. or 20 (6-oz.) servings.

PRIDE OF IOWA BARBECUE

Honey-barbecued Pork Chops*

Parslied Rice

Fresh Fruit Salad*

Cottage Cheese Rolls*

Iced Mocha Float*

Honey-barbecued Pork Chops

½ c. honey
½ c. ketchup
½ c. chili sauce
¼ c. finely chopped green pepper
¼ c. finely chopped onion
2 tblsp. cider vinegar
1 tblsp. prepared mustard
1 tblsp. Worcestershire sauce
2 drops Tabasco sauce
6 pork chops, ¾" thick
salt
pepper

IN ADVANCE:
Combine honey, ketchup, chili sauce, green pepper, onion, vinegar, mustard, Worcestershire and Tabasco in 2-qt. saucepan. Cook over high heat until mixture comes to a boil. Reduce heat to low. Simmer 30 minutes.

Pour sauce into glass bowl, cover and refrigerate.

TO GRILL:
Season pork chops with salt and pepper. Grill chops 4" from gray coals (medium heat), turning and basting often with marinade. Cook 1 hour or until no longer pink in center. Makes 6 servings.

As any Iowan will tell you, pork tastes great cooked on the grill. Honey-barbecued Pork Chops are basted and glazed with a bright red sauce sweetened with honey. A bowl of fluffy rice dotted with parsley makes a nice companion. Homemade yeast dinner rolls are flecked with cottage cheese and baked to a mouth-watering golden brown. Our Fresh Fruit Salad is a colorful flavor combination of grapefruit and orange segments, bananas, pineapple and red grapes topped with cool orange sherbet and sprinkled with coconut—so refreshing on a hot summer's day.

Fresh Fruit Salad

4 oranges
2 pink grapefruit
1 pineapple, pared, cored and cut
  into 1" cubes
½ lb. red grapes, halved and seeded
2 bananas
1 pt. orange sherbet
½ c. flaked coconut

IN ADVANCE:

Peel oranges and grapefruit with a sharp knife, removing the white part of peel. Remove segments. Squeeze membranes to release juice into bowl. Add pineapple and grapes. Toss lightly to mix well. Cover and refrigerate.

TO SERVE:

Just before serving, slice bananas and add to fruit mixture. Toss lightly to mix well and spoon into serving dishes. Top with scoops of sherbet and sprinkle with coconut. Makes 6 servings.

Cottage Cheese Rolls

2 pkg. active dry yeast
½ c. lukewarm water (110°)
2 c. creamed cottage cheese
¼ c. sugar
2 tsp. salt
½ tsp. baking soda
2 eggs
4½ c. sifted flour

IN ADVANCE:

Sprinkle yeast on lukewarm water; stir to dissolve.

Heat cottage cheese until lukewarm. Combine cottage cheese, sugar, salt, baking soda, eggs, yeast mixture and 1 c. flour in bowl. Beat with an electric mixer at medium speed until smooth, about 2 minutes, scraping bowl occasionally.

Gradually add enough remaining flour to make a soft dough that leaves the sides of the bowl.

Place dough in greased bowl; turn over to grease top. Cover and let rise in warm place until doubled, about 1½ hours.

Turn dough out onto lightly floured surface. Divide dough into 24 sections. Shape each section into a ball. Place balls in 2 greased 9" round baking pans. Let rise until doubled, about 45 minutes.

Bake in 350° oven 20 minutes or until golden brown. Remove from pans; cool on rack. Makes 24 rolls.

Iced Mocha Float

6 c. fresh-perked coffee, chilled
6 tblsp. chocolate-flavored syrup
1 pt. vanilla ice cream

Combine coffee and chocolate-flavored syrup. Mix well. Pour into 6 (12-oz.) glasses and add 1 scoop of ice cream to each glass. Makes 6 servings.

FATHER'S DAY FAVORITES

Mixed Grill*

Ratatouille*

Crusty Rolls   Butter

Marble Squares à la Mode*

Raspberry-Lemon Fizz*

L*et Dad sleep a little later on his special day, watch his favorite sporting event on TV, and even read the newspaper. Then treat him to a Mixed Grill of tender rib lamb chops and breakfast sausage links wrapped in bacon. Serve it with Ratatouille—a colorful mélange of eggplant, zucchini, green peppers, tomatoes and onion that cooks on the grill. Club soda adds the fizz to a tart and tangy raspberry and lemon drink—a nice companion to Marble Squares à la Mode.*

Mixed Grill

1½ lb. sausage links (12)
12 strips bacon
6 lamb rib chops

IN ADVANCE:
   Wrap each sausage link with 1 strip bacon and secure with wooden picks. Cover and refrigerate.
TO GRILL:
   Cook sausages and lamb chops 4″ from gray coals (medium heat), turning often with tongs. Grill 20 to 25 minutes or until sausages are completely cooked and chops are well browned. Makes 6 servings.

Ratatouille

1 small eggplant, cut into ½″ cubes
3 small zucchini, sliced
2 large tomatoes, cut up
2 medium onions, thinly sliced
   and separated into rings
1 medium green pepper, cut into thin
   strips
2 cloves garlic, minced
¼ c. cooking oil
2 tblsp. chopped fresh parsley
½ tsp. salt
½ tsp. dried thyme leaves
¼ tsp. pepper
1 bay leaf

IN ADVANCE:
   Combine all ingredients on a 30″ length of heavy duty foil, mixing lightly but well. Securely wrap mixture into a loose packet and refrigerate.
TO GRILL:
   Cook vegetable packet 4″ from red-gray coals (high heat). Grill 1 hour, turning often, or until vegetables are tender. Makes 6 servings.

Marble Squares
à la Mode

⅔ c. sifted flour
½ tsp. baking powder
¼ tsp. salt
½ c. butter or regular margarine
¾ c. sugar
2 eggs
1½ tsp. vanilla
1 (1-oz.) square unsweetened chocolate,
  melted and cooled
Fudge Sauce (recipe follows)
vanilla ice cream

IN ADVANCE:

Sift together flour, baking powder and salt; set aside.

Cream together butter and sugar in bowl until light and fluffy, using an electric mixer at medium speed. Add eggs one at a time, beating well after each addition. Blend in vanilla.

Gradually add dry ingredients to creamed mixture, beating well after each addition, using an electric mixer at low speed.

Spoon half of cake mixture into another bowl. Stir in cooled chocolate. Drop chocolate mixture and vanilla mixture alternately (like a checker-board) in greased 8″ square baking pan. Zigzag metal spatula through batter to marble.

Bake in 350° oven 25 to 30 minutes, or until cake tester or wooden pick inserted in center comes out clean. Cool in pan on rack. Cut into squares. Makes 9 servings.

TO SERVE:

Prepare Fudge Sauce. Top each cake square with a scoop of vanilla ice cream and spoon Fudge Sauce over top.

FUDGE SAUCE: Combine ¾ c. sugar, 3 tblsp. baking cocoa and dash of salt in 2-qt. saucepan. Blend in 2 tblsp. water, stirring until cocoa is dissolved. Stir in ⅔ c. evaporated milk. Cook over medium heat, stirring constantly, until mixture comes to a boil.

Boil over low heat 3 to 4 minutes, stirring constantly, until sauce thickens. Remove from heat. Stir in 2 tblsp. butter or regular margarine and 1 tsp. vanilla. Cool to lukewarm. Makes 1 c.

Raspberry-Lemon Fizz

1 (3-oz.) pkg. raspberry-flavored gelatin
⅓ c. sugar
2 c. boiling water
1 (6-oz.) can frozen lemonade concentrate
3 c. iced water
⅓ c. lemon juice
1 (28-oz.) bottle club soda, chilled

IN ADVANCE:

Dissolve gelatin and sugar in boiling water in large bowl. Add frozen lemonade concentrate and iced water, stirring until thawed. Stir in lemon juice. Cover and refrigerate.

TO SERVE:

Stir club soda into juice mixture. Serve over ice cubes in tall glasses. Makes 6 (12-oz.) servings.

Italian Sausage Kabobs*

Overnight Tossed Green Salad*

Bacon-Onion Rolls*

Melonade Cooler*

Italian Sausage Kabobs are among our favorite no-fuss recipes; they're made by skewering fresh mushrooms, cherry tomatoes and chunks of green pepper. You won't shed any tears peeling onions for the crusty Bacon-Onion Rolls because the onion flavor comes from a packaged soup mix. Serve the rolls with a chilled plate of Overnight Tossed Green Salad—you'll spend more time relaxing before dinner because the salad is assembled and "dressed" a day in advance. An Arizona farm woman developed this recipe for Melonade Cooler, a refreshing beverage with the sunny taste of summer.

Italian Sausage Kabobs

2 lb. sweet Italian sausage, cut
  into 1" slices
1 lb. fresh mushrooms
18 cherry tomatoes
1 green pepper, cut into 1" chunks
  cooking oil

IN ADVANCE:
  Alternately thread sausage, mushrooms, tomatoes and green pepper onto 6 (12") skewers. Cover and refrigerate.
TO GRILL:
  Cook kabobs 4" from gray coals (medium heat), turning and basting often with oil. Cook 35 to 40 minutes or until sausage is browned and vegetables are tender. Makes 6 kabobs.

Overnight Tossed Green Salad

1 medium head iceberg lettuce
1 (10-oz.) pkg. fresh spinach
½ c. sliced green onions
1 pt. cherry tomatoes, halved
1 (10-oz.) pkg. frozen peas, thawed
1 lb. bacon, diced, cooked and drained
1½ c. mayonnaise
1 c. dairy sour cream
2 tblsp. lemon juice
½ tsp. dried oregano leaves
¼ tsp. dried basil leaves
¼ tsp. salt
⅛ tsp. pepper

IN ADVANCE:
  Tear lettuce and spinach into bite-sized pieces in a very large salad bowl. Add onions, tomatoes, peas and bacon; toss lightly to mix well. Set aside.
  Combine remaining ingredients in another bowl. Mix well. Spread dressing

over greens; be sure to "frost" entire surface (but do not mix). Cover with plastic wrap and refrigerate overnight.

TO SERVE:

Toss dressing with greens. Makes 8 servings.

Bacon-Onion Rolls

8 strips bacon
4½ to 4¾ c. sifted flour
¼ c. dry onion soup mix
2 pkg. active dry yeast
1 tblsp. sugar
1½ c. beer
¼ c. milk
1 tblsp. butter or regular margarine
2 tblsp. butter or regular margarine,
    melted
1 tblsp. corn meal

IN ADVANCE:

Fry bacon in 10″ skillet over medium heat about 5 minutes or until crisp. Remove with slotted spoon; drain on paper towels and crumble. Set aside. Reserve 2 tblsp. bacon drippings.

Stir together 1¾ c. of the flour, onion soup mix, undissolved yeast and sugar in mixing bowl.

Heat beer, milk, reserved 2 tblsp. bacon drippings and 1 tblsp. butter in 1-qt. saucepan over low heat until very warm (120-130°). (Mixture will look curdled.) Pour over flour-yeast mixture all at once.

Beat ½ minute, using an electric mixer at low speed. Turn to high speed and beat 3 minutes more. Stir in crumbled bacon and enough remaining flour to make a soft dough.

Turn dough out onto floured surface. Knead until smooth and elastic, about 5 minutes. Place in greased bowl, turning over once to grease top. Cover and let rise in warm place until doubled, about 45 minutes.

Punch down dough. Divide into 18 sections. Let rest 10 minutes. Shape each section into a ball. Place balls in greased 3″ muffin-pan cups. Cover and let rise in warm place until doubled, about 30 minutes.

Brush tops of rolls with 2 tblsp. melted butter. Sprinkle with corn meal.

Bake in 375° oven 18 minutes or until golden brown. Remove from pan. Cool completely and wrap in foil, or serve immediately. Makes 18.

TO REHEAT:

Warm foil-wrapped rolls on grill.

Melonade Cooler

1 (5-lb.) section of watermelon
¼ c. sugar
3 tblsp. lemon juice
lemon-lime flavored soda, chilled
1 qt. lime sherbet
12 fresh strawberries

IN ADVANCE:

Scoop pulp from watermelon; remove seeds. Purée half of the watermelon in blender or food processor; pour into bowl. Repeat with remaining watermelon. Add to purée in bowl (you should have 4 c. purée). Stir in sugar and lemon juice. Mix well. Cover and refrigerate.

TO SERVE:

Pour ⅓ c. purée mixture in each of 6 (12-oz.) glasses. Refrigerate remaining 2 c. purée and reserve for seconds. Pour lemon-lime soda to within 1″ of top of glass. Top with a scoop of lime sherbet. Garnish each glass with a strawberry. Makes 6 servings plus seconds.

Kansas-style Beef Tacos*

Guacamole Salad*

Easy Fresh Blueberry Cake*

Limeade*

The rancher's wife who developed this recipe says that Kansas-style Beef Tacos can be made with leftover roast beef, steak, hamburger patties and even meat loaf. Guacamole Salad is a savory, festive salad topped with a dressing of avocados, tomato and green pepper, spiced with chili powder and Tabasco. The dressing also makes a wonderful dip. A frosty Limeade is refreshingly good with the Easy Fresh Blueberry Cake—a crumb-topped cake with a blueberry center. It has a cake mix base and mixes up in minutes.

Kansas-style Beef Tacos

2 (14½-oz.) cans stewed tomatoes
2 cloves garlic
1 tblsp. vinegar
2 tblsp. chili powder
2 tsp. dried oregano leaves
1 tsp. salt
1 tsp. ground cumin
¼ tsp. pepper
½ c. water
4 c. chopped cooked beef
16 taco shells
condiments: shredded lettuce, chopped tomato, sliced avocado, sliced ripe olives, chopped onion, chopped chili peppers and shredded Cheddar cheese

IN ADVANCE:
Combine stewed tomatoes, garlic, vinegar, chili powder, oregano, salt, cumin, pepper and water in blender jar. Cover and blend at high speed until smooth. Pour mixture into bowl; cover and refrigerate.

TO COOK:
Combine beef and tomato mixture in 12″ skillet. Simmer, uncovered, over low heat 35 minutes or until mixture thickens. Remove from heat.

Fill each taco shell with ¼ c. meat mixture and top with condiments of your choice. Makes 16 tacos.

Guacamole Salad

1 tomato, peeled and chopped
⅓ c. finely chopped green pepper
2 tblsp. finely chopped green onion
2 tblsp. lemon juice
½ tsp. chili powder
½ tsp. salt
¼ tsp. Tabasco sauce
dash pepper
2 ripe avocados
6 c. shredded lettuce
1 tomato, peeled and chopped
1 c. shredded Cheddar cheese
½ c. sliced, pitted black olives

IN ADVANCE:

Combine 1 tomato, green pepper, green onion, lemon juice, chili powder, salt, Tabasco sauce and pepper in bowl; mix well. Set aside.

Peel avocados and remove pits. Mash avocados with fork. Add avocados to tomato mixture. Mix well. Cover surface of avocado-tomato mixture with plastic wrap and refrigerate at least 1 hour before serving.

Cover and refrigerate.

Meanwhile, place lettuce, 1 tomato, cheese and olives in salad bowl.

TO SERVE:

Toss lettuce and tomato mixture lightly to mix well. Top with avocado-tomato mixture. Makes 8 servings.

Easy Fresh Blueberry Cake

1 (18½-oz.) pkg. yellow cake mix
⅔ c. water
1 egg
¼ c. butter or regular margarine, melted
1 tsp. ground cinnamon
⅛ tsp. ground nutmeg
1½ c. fresh blueberries

Measure 2 c. cake mix in bowl and set aside. Prepare remaining mix according to package directions, adding water and egg. Measure 1 c. batter; set aside. Pour remaining batter into greased 9″ square baking pan.

Combine reserved 2 c. cake mix, butter, cinnamon and nutmeg in bowl. Mix until crumbly. Sprinkle half of the crumb mixture evenly over batter in pan. Arrange blueberries evenly over crumb mixture. Spoon reserved batter evenly over top of blueberries. Sprinkle with remaining half of crumb mixture.

Bake in 350° oven 45 to 50 minutes or until done. Serve warm. Makes 8 servings.

Limeade

2 limes
1⅓ c. sugar
1 c. water
1¼ c. fresh lime juice
5½ c. iced water

IN ADVANCE:

Using a vegetable parer, thinly peel rind from limes; cut rind into strips.

Combine sugar, 1 c. water and lime rind in 2-qt. saucepan. Heat to a boil over high heat. Reduce heat to medium and boil 5 minutes.

Remove from heat and strain. Stir in lime juice. Pour into 2½-qt. heatproof pitcher or bowl. Cover and refrigerate.

TO SERVE:

Stir in iced water and serve over ice. Makes 2 qt. or 8 (8-oz.) servings.

Chicken Livers wrapped in Bacon*

Louise's Luau Spareribs*

Mixed Vegetable Kabobs*

Green Salad   Zesty Tomato Dressing*

Fresh Pineapple

With a big imagination, it's easy to go from plain hamburgers to a luau cookout, says a Tennessee farm woman. This luau for six is built around Louise's Luau Spareribs. The gingery, peach-based barbecue sauce glazes the ribs and gives them a hint of oriental flavor. For a great taste sensation, start the cookout by nibbling on chicken livers and crunchy water chestnuts encircled by crisp bacon. Then thread your favorite vegetables on skewers and baste with herb dressing as they grill.

Chicken Livers wrapped in Bacon

1 lb. (about 15) chicken livers, cut in half
1 (8-oz.) can water chestnuts, drained
    and cut in half
¼ c. soy sauce
1 tblsp. sugar
1 small clove garlic, minced
⅛ tsp. ground ginger
15 strips bacon

IN ADVANCE:
    Combine chicken livers, water chestnuts, soy sauce, sugar, garlic and ginger in bowl. Marinate for 30 minutes.
    Meanwhile, partially cook bacon in skillet over medium heat. Remove from skillet and cut in half. Holding 1 chicken liver half and 1 water chestnut half together, wrap one-half bacon strip around the two. Secure with a wooden pick. Repeat with remaining ingredients and refrigerate.

TO GRILL:
    Cook chicken livers 4″ from gray coals (medium heat), turning often. Cook 6 to 10 minutes or until bacon crisps and chicken livers are cooked. Makes 30 appetizers.

Louise's Luau Spareribs

2 (4½-oz.) jars strained peaches
½ c. brown sugar, packed
⅓ c. ketchup
⅓ c. vinegar
2 tblsp. soy sauce
2 tsp. ground ginger
1 clove garlic, minced
⅛ tsp. pepper
5 lb. country-style pork ribs

IN ADVANCE:

Combine peaches, brown sugar, ketchup, vinegar, soy sauce, ginger, garlic and pepper in a 2-qt. saucepan. Cook over medium heat until mixture comes to a boil. Reduce heat to low. Simmer 5 minutes.

Pour sauce into glass bowl, cover and refrigerate.

TO GRILL:

Cook pork ribs 4″ from gray coals (medium heat), turning and basting often with sauce. Cook 1 hour or until no longer pink in center. Makes 6 servings.

Mixed Vegetable Kabobs

1 (1-lb.) eggplant, cut into 1″ cubes
2 small zucchini, cut into 1″ slices
2 small summer squash, cut into 1″ slices
1 large green pepper, cut into 1″ squares
12 fresh medium mushroom caps
1 pt. cherry tomatoes
1 (8-oz.) bottle herb-flavored
   or Italian salad dressing

IN ADVANCE:

Alternately thread eggplant, zucchini, summer squash, green pepper and mushrooms on 4 (12″) skewers. Set aside. Thread cherry tomatoes on 2 (12″) skewers. Cover and refrigerate.

TO GRILL:

Cook the 4 mixed vegetable kabobs 4″ from gray coals (medium heat), turning and basting often with dressing. Cook 10 minutes.

Add tomato kabobs to grill and cook for 10 minutes alongside other kabobs, turning often and basting with dressing.

To serve, baste each kabob generously with dressing. Makes 6 to 8 servings.

Zesty Tomato Dressing

½ c. salad oil
⅓ c. cider vinegar
1 (8-oz.) can tomato sauce
½ tsp. salt
2 tblsp. sugar
1 tsp. dry mustard
1 tsp. paprika
½ tsp. dried oregano leaves
2 tsp. Worcestershire sauce
½ clove garlic, minced
2 tsp. finely chopped onion
1 tblsp. finely chopped celery
2 tblsp. salad dressing

IN ADVANCE:

Combine all ingredients in small mixing bowl. Beat 2 minutes, using an electric mixer at medium speed (or blend for 15 seconds in a blender at high speed). Cover and refrigerate. Makes 1 pt.

Grilled Hamburgers*   Buns

Assorted Toppings

Eggciting Potato Salad*

Coleslaw Pepper Cups*

Outdoor Brownies*

Iced Coffee

W*hen it comes to cooking and eating out-of-doors, nothing is more taste-tempting than good ground beef hamburgers sizzling on the grill, a big bowl of potato salad, coleslaw-stuffed peppers and a plate full of chewy chocolate brownies—it's hard to beat the basics. Grilled Hamburgers are sure to be to everybody's liking if you serve a variety of interesting toppings. An Iowa farm woman shares her recipe for Eggciting Potato Salad, first prepared in her own kitchen by a Brazilian exchange student staying with her family. She adapted the recipe to accommodate locally available ingredients. Even the brownies can be baked outdoors if you have a covered grill.*

Grilled Hamburgers

2 lb. ground beef
½ c. ketchup
2 tsp. dry mustard
2 tsp. Worcestershire sauce
1 tsp. seasoned salt

IN ADVANCE:
Combine all ingredients in bowl. Mix lightly, but well. Form mixture into 8 (3″) patties and refrigerate.
TO GRILL:
Cook patties 4″ from gray coals (medium heat). Grill 4 to 5 minutes on each side. Makes 8 servings.

Eggciting Potato Salad

1 c. mayonnaise or salad dressing
⅓ c. Italian salad dressing
1 tsp. prepared mustard
¾ tsp. salt
⅛ tsp. pepper
⅛ tsp. Worcestershire sauce
¾ c. chopped celery
½ c. diced, cooked carrots
½ c. sliced radishes
¼ c. cooked peas
¼ c. chopped onion
1 medium tomato, peeled and diced
3 hard-cooked eggs, chopped
¼ c. chopped fresh parsley
6 c. cubed, cooked potatoes

IN ADVANCE:
Combine mayonnaise, Italian salad dressing, mustard, salt, pepper and Worcestershire sauce in large bowl. Mix well. Fold in celery, carrots, radishes, peas, onion, tomato, eggs and parsley. Gently stir in potatoes. Cover and refrigerate at least 3 hours before serving. Makes 10 c. or 8 servings.

Coleslaw Pepper Cups

1 c. cider vinegar
1 c. sugar
2 tblsp. chopped pimiento
¼ tsp. celery seeds
¼ tsp. dry mustard
¼ tsp. salt
⅛ tsp. pepper
4 c. shredded cabbage
1 c. shredded, pared carrots
½ c. chopped radishes
¼ c. finely chopped onion
4 large green peppers

IN ADVANCE:
Combine vinegar, sugar, pimiento, celery seeds, mustard, salt and pepper in bowl. Mix well. Set aside. Combine cabbage, carrots, radishes and onion in another bowl. Pour dressing over cabbage mixture. Toss lightly to mix well. Cover and refrigerate.

TO SERVE:
Cut green peppers in half lengthwise. Remove seeds. Spoon an equal amount of cabbage slaw into each pepper half. Makes 8 servings.

Outdoor Brownies

½ c. butter or regular margarine
2 (1-oz.) squares unsweetened chocolate
1 c. sugar
2 eggs
1 tsp. vanilla
⅔ c. flour
½ c. chopped walnuts

IN ADVANCE:
Using heavy-duty foil, construct a heat deflector (see p. 6).

TO GRILL:
Place heat deflector on the grill. Preheat grill and reduce temperature to low.

Combine butter and chocolate in 2-qt. saucepan. Cook over low heat or over low coals until melted.

Remove from heat and stir in sugar. Mix well. Add eggs, one at a time, beating well after each addition. Blend in vanilla. Add flour and mix well. Stir in walnuts.

Spread mixture in greased 8″ square baking pan. Place on heat deflector.

Close lid and bake at low heat 25 minutes or until done. Cool in baking pan on rack. Cut into 2″ squares. Makes 16 squares.

Roaster on a Spit
with Curried Stuffing*

Red, White and Blue Gelatin Ring*

Refrigerated Yeast Rolls*

Grilled Whole Pineapple*

Vanilla Ice Cream

Your Independence Day celebration will have a patriotic show of colors with a Red, White and Blue Gelatin Ring. Each layer has a distinctive flavor that blends well with the others. For an entrée, break the holiday hot dog-and-hamburger habit and show your own independence by serving Roaster on a Spit with Curried Stuffing. Warm the crescent rolls on the grill and serve them with herbed butter. A fresh whole pineapple studded with cloves and glazed with brown sugar cooks unattended on the spit while you enjoy the party.

Roaster on a Spit with Curried Stuffing

1 c. chopped, pared apple
½ c. chopped onion
⅓ c. chopped celery
⅓ c. chopped green pepper
¼ c. butter or regular margarine
4 c. bread cubes (½" cubes)
¼ c. milk
1 to 2 tsp. curry powder
½ tsp. salt
¼ tsp. pepper
1 (6 to 7-lb.) roasting chicken

IN ADVANCE:

Sauté apple, onion, celery and green pepper in butter in 10" skillet over medium heat until tender. Remove from heat. Add bread cubes, milk, curry powder, salt and pepper. Toss lightly to mix well. Place mixture in bowl. Cover and refrigerate.

TO GRILL:

Loosely stuff cavity of roaster with stuffing mixture. Close cavity and secure with skewers. Truss. Run spit through center of roaster. Set spit forks in breast and thighs; tighten. Holding spit at both ends, turn. If one side drops downward, reposition so it is balanced. Securely tie wings and legs to body.

Place on gas grill rotisserie, close lid and grill over low heat. Cook 2 to 2½ hours or until meat thermometer inserted in stuffing registers 165°. Makes 6 servings.

Red, White and Blue Gelatin Ring

1 (3-oz.) pkg. strawberry-flavored gelatin
1 (10-oz.) pkg. frozen strawberries, thawed
1 (3-oz.) pkg. lemon-flavored gelatin

¾ c. dairy sour cream
1 (3-oz.) pkg. cherry-flavored gelatin
1½ c. blueberries, fresh or frozen

IN ADVANCE:

Combine strawberry gelatin and 1 c. boiling water in bowl, stirring until gelatin dissolves. Stir in strawberries and their juice. Pour into 6-c. ring mold. Refrigerate 1 hour or until set.

Combine lemon gelatin and 1 c. boiling water in bowl, stirring until gelatin dissolves. Add sour cream, mixing until blended and smooth. Pour on top of set strawberry layer. Refrigerate 1 hour or until set.

Combine cherry gelatin and 1 c. boiling water in bowl, stirring until gelatin dissolves. Stir in blueberries. Refrigerate until syrupy. Pour on top of set lemon layer. Refrigerate 1 hour or until set. Makes 6 servings.

Refrigerated Yeast Rolls

1 c. boiling water
¾ c. lard or shortening
½ c. sugar
¾ tsp. salt
1 pkg. active dry yeast
½ c. lukewarm water (110°)
6½ c. sifted flour
1 c. prepared instant mashed potatoes
2 eggs

IN ADVANCE:

Combine boiling water, lard, sugar and salt in large mixing bowl. Cool to lukewarm. Sprinkle yeast over lukewarm water; stir until yeast dissolves.

Add yeast mixture, 1 c. of the flour, mashed potatoes and eggs to lard mixture. Beat with an electric mixer at medium speed until smooth, about 2 minutes. Gradually stir in remaining flour. (No kneading is necessary).

Place dough in greased 4-qt. bowl. Grease top of dough. Cover with aluminum foil. Refrigerate at least 2 hours, or up to 1 week.

Punch down dough. Divide dough into fourths. Let rest 10 minutes.

Roll out each fourth to 12″ circle. Cut into 12 wedges. Roll up each wedge, starting at the wide end. Place point side down on greased baking sheets, about 3″ apart. Shape into crescents.

Cover and let rise in warm place until almost doubled, about 45 minutes.

Bake in 375° oven 15 minutes or until golden brown. Remove from baking sheets. Cool completely and wrap in foil, or serve immediately. Makes 4 doz. rolls.

Grilled Whole Pineapple

1 fresh pineapple
whole cloves
¼ c. butter or regular margarine
¼ c. brown sugar, packed

Leaving leafy crown intact, pare pineapple. Remove eyes. Score pineapple in diamond pattern and place a clove in the center of each diamond.

TO GRILL:

Remove a few leaves from the center of the pineapple's crown. Work rotisserie spit into the center of the crown and through the entire length of the pineapple. Secure bottom of pineapple with holding fork. Wrap leafy crown well in foil. Grill on rotisserie over gray coals (medium heat) 30 minutes.

Heat butter and brown sugar in saucepan until butter is melted. Brush mixture evenly over pineapple. Cook 15 minutes longer or until pineapple is well glazed. Remove foil. Remove pineapple from spit and slice. Makes 6 servings.

BLOCK PARTY BARBECUE

Ginger-glazed Spareribs*

Macaroni-Egg Salad Supreme*

Herbed Corn on the Grill*

Orange Sherbet Molds
with Strawberries*

Ribs are a favorite with everyone, and each savory bite of these Ginger-glazed Spareribs offers a contrast of sweet-sour flavors and tender-crispy textures. This recipe for Macaroni-Egg Salad Supreme was shared by one Illinois woman who's been making it for community picnics over the past 25 summers. "The men barbecue the ribs and the women bring their favorite recipes," she says. Herbed Corn on the Grill is seasoned with herbed butter. Top off the meal with individual molds of frosty orange sherbet capped with plump fresh strawberries.

Ginger-glazed Spareribs

6 lb. pork spareribs
water
1 c. sugar
2 tblsp. cornstarch
2 tsp. salt
1 tsp. ground ginger
½ tsp. pepper
⅔ c. lemon juice
½ c. soy sauce
½ c. water

IN ADVANCE:

Place ribs in a large kettle with enough water to cover. Cook over high heat until mixture comes to a boil. Reduce heat to low and simmer 45 minutes or until tender. Drain and set aside.

Combine sugar, cornstarch, salt, ginger and pepper in 2-qt. saucepan. Stir in lemon juice, soy sauce and ½ c. water. Cook over high heat until mixture comes to a boil.

Reduce heat to medium and cook 3 minutes. Remove from heat.

TO GRILL:

Cook ribs 4" from gray coals (medium heat), turning and basting often with glaze. Cook 20 minutes or until glazed and nicely browned. Makes 8 servings.

Macaroni-Egg Salad Supreme

2 c. elbow macaroni, cooked and drained
1½ c. chopped celery
1 (8¼-oz.) can crushed pineapple, drained
1 c. shredded pasteurized process
  American cheese
7 hard-cooked eggs, chopped
¾ c. mayonnaise
½ c. chopped green peppcr
3 tblsp. chopped pimiento
2 tblsp. grated Parmesan cheese
½ tsp. salt

IN ADVANCE:
Combine all ingredients in bowl. Toss lightly to mix well. Cover and refrigerate at least several hours before serving. Makes 10 c. or 8 servings.

Herbed Corn on the Grill

½ c. butter or regular margarine, softened
2 tblsp. chopped fresh parsley
2 tblsp. chopped chives, fresh or
  freeze-dried
¼ tsp. garlic salt
⅛ tsp. pepper
8 ears fresh corn, husked

IN ADVANCE:
Combine butter, parsley, chives, garlic salt and pepper in bowl. Mix well.
Spread each ear with butter mixture and place on a 12″ length of heavy-duty foil. Securely wrap each ear into a loose packet and refrigerate.
TO GRILL:
Cook corn 4″ from gray coals (medium heat), turning often. Cook 20 to 30 minutes or until corn is tender. Makes 8 servings.

Orange Sherbet Molds with Strawberries

1 qt. orange sherbet or ice
1 qt. fresh strawberries
¼ c. orange juice, chilled
¼ c. ginger ale, chilled

IN ADVANCE:
Stir orange sherbet in bowl until softened, using a spoon. Rinse 8 individual molds with iced water. Spoon softened orange sherbet into molds. Freeze until firm. (Or place scoops of orange sherbet on baking sheet and freeze until firm.)
Hull strawberries and refrigerate until serving time. Place dessert plates in freezer until very cold.
TO SERVE:
Unmold orange sherbet onto chilled dessert plates by wrapping a cloth dipped in warm water around each mold. Spoon ½ c. strawberries over each serving.
Mix together orange juice and ginger ale and pour 1 tblsp. of the mixture over each serving. Makes 8 servings.

Pioneer Drumsticks*

Barbecued Corn*

Baked Potatoes with Cheddar Cheese*

S'mores*

Here's a do-it-yourself meal that lets everyone sit back and enjoy being out-of-doors while the potatoes bake. When it's time to roast the corn and grill the meat, give each campfire chef a wooden skewer to spear Pioneer Drumsticks—lightly spiced individual mini-meat loaves. The ears of corn are painted with a tangy barbecue sauce and cook unattended in a little less time than the meat. Even the dessert is made with the heat of the coals; if you've never tasted these graham cracker sandwiches with their centers of chocolate and toasted marshmallow, you'll know as soon as you take a bite how they got their name—you're sure to want S'more.

Pioneer Drumsticks

1½ lb. ground chuck
2 c. cornflakes
¼ c. ketchup
1 egg, slightly beaten
1 tsp. Worcestershire sauce
¼ tsp. salt
⅛ tsp. pepper

IN ADVANCE:
Combine all ingredients in bowl. Mix lightly but well.
Divide mixture into 6 equal portions. Shape each portion into a log shape. Insert a 10″ wooden skewer lengthwise into each. Cover and refrigerate.
TO GRILL:
Cook drumsticks 4″ from gray coals (medium heat), turning often. Grill 20 to 25 minutes or to desired doneness. Makes 6 servings.

Barbecued Corn

¾ c. ketchup
4 tblsp. butter or regular margarine
2 tblsp. wine vinegar
1 tblsp. brown sugar, packed
1 tblsp. molasses
2 tsp. dry mustard
1 tsp. Worcestershire sauce
½ tsp. onion salt
¼ tsp. Tabasco sauce
6 ears fresh corn, husked

IN ADVANCE:
Combine all ingredients except corn in a 1-qt. saucepan. Cook over high heat until mixture comes to a boil.

Reduce heat to low. Simmer 5 minutes. Remove from heat and set aside.

Place each ear of corn on a 12″ length of heavy-duty foil. Spoon the sauce equally over each ear. Securely wrap each ear into a loose packet and refrigerate.

TO GRILL:
Cook corn 4″ from gray coals (medium heat), turning often. Grill 20 to 30 minutes or until corn is tender. Makes 6 servings.

Baked Potatoes with Cheddar Cheese

6 medium baking potatoes
¾ c. shredded Cheddar cheese

IN ADVANCE:
Wash potatoes and dry well. Prick each potato several times with a fork. Wrap each potato in a 12″ square of heavy-duty foil. Set aside at room temperature.

TO GRILL:
Cook potatoes 6″ from gray coals (medium heat). Grill 45 minutes or until tender, turning occasionally.

Unwrap potatoes and cut a 1½″ cross in the top of each. Holding ends, press toward center, until white part of potato bursts through cross. Sprinkle with cheese. Makes 6 servings.

S'mores

12 marshmallows
2 (2-oz.) milk chocolate bars
12 (2″ square) graham crackers

TO GRILL:
For each serving, press 2 marshmallows on the tines of a long-handled fork or a green twig. Hold marshmallows 4″ over gray coals (medium heat), turning often. Cook until golden brown and puffy.

Place one-third of a chocolate bar on 1 graham cracker square. Slide toasted marshmallows onto the chocolate and top with another graham cracker square. Makes 6 servings.

MIDSUMMER NIGHT'S SUPPER

Cucumber Dip*

Assorted Fresh Vegetable Dippers

Layered Salmon Salad*

Health Crackers*

Ice Cream 'n' Pretzel Pie*

Orange-Cider Punch*

When appetites begin to wane on a sultry midsummer's eve, organize a light summer supper around foods that are cool and crisp. Serve creamy chilled Cucumber Dip surrounded by a relish tray of crunchy raw vegetable dippers and a dish of crisp homemade Health Crackers. The crackers are made with oats and wheat germ for extra nutrition. Layered Salmon Salad is sure to perk up appetites—it looks wonderful with the lettuce, macaroni, green olives, tomatoes, cucumbers and chunks of flaky salmon layered in a rainbow of colors. You can put some pizazz in the refreshing Orange-Cider Punch by adding a garnish of fresh fruit.

Cucumber Dip

1 (8-oz.) pkg. cream cheese, softened
¾ c. grated cucumber
2 tsp. finely chopped green pepper
1½ tsp. grated onion
2 tblsp. lemon juice
¼ tsp. salt
⅛ tsp. pepper

IN ADVANCE:
Combine all ingredients in bowl. Mix well. Cover and refrigerate. Makes 1½ c.
TO SERVE:
Serve dip with crackers or an assortment of fresh vegetables.

Layered Salmon Salad

1½ c. mayonnaise
¼ c. bottled Italian salad dressing
1 tblsp. finely chopped onion
½ tsp. dill
2 c. shredded lettuce
2 c. seashell macaroni, cooked and drained
½ c. sliced pimiento-stuffed green olives
2 c. chopped tomatoes
2 c. sliced cucumbers
1 (15½-oz.) can salmon, drained, boned and flaked
paprika
chopped fresh parsley

IN ADVANCE:
Combine mayonnaise, Italian salad dressing, onion and dill in bowl. Mix well. Cover and refrigerate at least 2 hours.
Meanwhile, in a large clear bowl, layer lettuce, macaroni, olives, tomatoes, cucumbers and salmon. Cover and refrigerate.

TO SERVE:

Cover entire surface of salad with mayonnaise mixture. Sprinkle with paprika and chopped parsley. Makes 6 servings.

Health Crackers

3 c. quick-cooking oats
2 c. unsifted flour
1 c. raw wheat germ
3 tblsp. sugar
1 tsp. salt
¾ c. cooking oil
1 c. water
1 egg white, slightly beaten
sesame or poppy seeds
garlic or onion salt

IN ADVANCE:

Combine oats, flour, wheat germ, sugar and salt in bowl. Add oil and water, stirring until mixture leaves the sides of the bowl. Divide dough into quarters. Set aside.

Roll out each quarter on a lightly floured surface to 12x10″ rectangle. Roll dough up loosely around rolling pin and place on lightly greased baking sheet. Cut into squares, triangles, rectangles or diamonds. Brush with egg white. Sprinkle with sesame seeds and garlic salt.

Bake in 350° oven 15 to 20 minutes or until golden brown. Remove from baking sheets; cool on racks. Makes about 8 doz. crackers.

Ice Cream 'n' Pretzel Pie

Pretzel Crust (recipe follows)
½ c. semisweet chocolate pieces, melted
½ gal. vanilla fudge ice cream, slightly softened

IN ADVANCE:

Prepare Pretzel Crust.

Spread melted chocolate pieces over bottom of Pretzel Crust. Freeze 10 minutes or until chocolate is set. Spoon or scoop ice cream over chocolate layer. Freeze until firm.

Wrap securely in heavy-duty foil. Return to freezer and continue freezing at least 8 hours or until ready to serve.

TO SERVE:

Remove pie from freezer 10 to 15 minutes before serving. Makes 6 servings.

PRETZEL CRUST: Combine 1½ c. coarsely crushed pretzel rods and ½ c. butter or regular margarine (softened), in bowl. Mix well. Press mixture into bottom and up sides of 9″ pie plate. Freeze at least 1 hour.

Orange-Cider Punch

1 qt. apple cider
2 c. orange juice
½ c. lemon juice
¼ c. sugar

IN ADVANCE:

Combine all ingredients in 2-qt. pitcher. Stir to mix well. Cover and refrigerate.

TO SERVE:

Pour punch over ice cubes in glasses. Makes about 6½ c. or 13 (4-oz.) servings.

Kielbasa and Mushroom Suppers*

Johnnycake*

Orange-Coconut-Apple Crisp*

Lemony Iced Tea*

In order to get a little more vacation fun out of the short summer season, many families drive to a nearby beach, lakefront or mountain trail loaded down with all they need— especially plenty of food. Foods that can be made ahead or cooked over a grill usually work best. The Kielbasa and Mushroom Suppers require no seasoning. Johnnycake is a skillet corn bread that can cook alongside the main dish; pre-measure dry ingredients in a plastic bag for easy mixing at the campsite. Orange-Coconut-Apple Crisp can be cooked early in the day and rewarmed on the grill, and a thermos of spiced tea chilled with lemon ice cubes will quench any thirst.

Kielbasa and Mushroom Suppers

2 lb. kielbasa
1 lb. fresh mushrooms, sliced
2 c. green pepper strips
1½ c. sliced onion

IN ADVANCE:
Divide kielbasa, mushrooms, green pepper and onion into 6 portions and layer each portion onto an 18″ length of heavy-duty foil.

Securely wrap each portion into a loose packet and refrigerate.

TO GRILL:
Cook packets 4″ from gray coals (medium heat) for 20 minutes. Turn and grill 20 minutes more. Makes 6 servings.

Johnnycake

1 c. sifted flour
1 c. yellow corn meal
¼ c. brown sugar, packed
4 tsp. baking powder
½ tsp. salt
1 c. milk
¼ c. cooking oil
1 egg, slightly beaten

IN ADVANCE:

Stir together flour, corn meal, brown sugar, baking powder and salt. Set aside.

Combine milk, oil and egg in bowl. Add dry ingredients, stirring just enough to moisten. Pour into greased, preheated 10″ skillet.

Cover and cook over low heat 30 minutes or until tester inserted in center comes out clean. Cool completely and wrap in foil (or serve immediately). Makes 8 servings.

TO REHEAT:

Warm foil-wrapped bread on grill.

Orange-Coconut-Apple Crisp

6 c. sliced, pared apples
2 tblsp. orange juice
⅔ c. brown sugar, packed
⅓ c. flour
½ tsp. grated orange rind
⅓ c. butter or regular margarine
1 c. flaked coconut
1 c. heavy cream

IN ADVANCE:

Arrange apples in 8″ square glass baking dish. Sprinkle with orange juice. Set aside.

Combine brown sugar, flour and orange rind in bowl. Cut in butter with pastry blender or two forks until mixture is crumbly. Add coconut and toss to mix well. Sprinkle over apples.

Bake in 375° oven 35 minutes.

TO SERVE:

Spoon into dessert dishes and pour heavy cream over each serving. Makes 6 servings.

Lemony Iced Tea

1 qt. lemonade
1 lemon
1 orange
8 whole cloves
1 (2″) cinnamon stick
4 tea bags
2 qt. boiling water

IN ADVANCE:

Fill ice cube trays with lemonade and freeze.

Using a vegetable parer, thinly peel rind from lemon and orange; cut rinds into strips. Combine rinds, cloves, cinnamon stick and tea bags in 2½-qt. heatproof pitcher or bowl. Add boiling water and steep 20 minutes. Strain.

Cover and refrigerate several hours before serving.

TO SERVE:

Place lemonade ice cubes in glasses and fill glasses with tea mixture. Set aside for 5 minutes to allow ice cubes to melt slightly. Just before serving, stir. Makes 2 qt. or 6 (10-oz.) servings.

Saucy Ribs*

Basil Beans and Tomatoes*

Fruity Rice Salad*

Hard-Hat Ice Cream Sundaes*

When the temperature soars
and cooking seems out of the question,
move out into the open air, where an
efficient outdoor kitchen can be
organized in a moment. Cook the
spareribs over medium coals, basting
them with a tangy tomato-based sauce.
Two farm-fresh favorites are teamed in
a colorful and flavorful side dish of
Basil Beans and Tomatoes; you can
cook this in a skillet right on the grill.
For a sweet and delicious grill-side
salad, try Fruity Rice Salad. Hard-Hat
Ice Cream Sundaes get their name from
the semisweet chocolate sauce that
hardens over the ice cream, forming a
shiny cap.

Saucy Ribs

6 lb. pork spareribs
1 tsp. salt
water
3 tblsp. cooking oil
⅓ c. finely chopped onion
1 clove garlic, minced
¾ c. ketchup
⅓ c. light corn syrup
⅓ c. cider vinegar
2 tblsp. Worcestershire sauce
2 tblsp. soy sauce
2 tblsp. spicy mustard

IN ADVANCE:
Place ribs and salt in a large kettle
with enough water to cover. Cook until
water comes to a boil. Reduce heat to
low. Simmer 45 minutes or until almost
tender.

Drain well and place ribs in bowl.
Cover and refrigerate. Meanwhile, heat
oil in 2-qt. saucepan over medium heat.
Add onion and garlic and sauté about 5
minutes or until tender.

Stir in ketchup, corn syrup, vinegar,
Worcestershire sauce, soy sauce and
mustard. Cook until mixture comes to a
boil. Reduce heat to low and simmer 15
minutes.

Pour sauce into bowl, cover and
refrigerate.

TO GRILL:
Cook ribs 4″ from gray coals
(medium heat), turning and basting
often with sauce. Grill 30 minutes or
until ribs are well glazed. Makes
6 servings.

Basil Beans
and Tomatoes

¼ c. cooking oil
2 lb. fresh green beans, bias-cut into
    1½" lengths
⅔ c. chopped onion
2 cloves garlic, minced
1 c. water
2 tsp. dried basil leaves
1 tsp. salt
¼ tsp. pepper
4 medium tomatoes, chopped

TO GRILL:

Heat oil in 12" skillet 4" from gray coals (medium heat).Add green beans, onion and garlic. Stir-fry 4 minutes. Add water, basil, salt and pepper. Cover and steam 20 minutes or until tender-crisp.

Stir in tomatoes. Cook, stirring constantly, 2 minutes. Makes 6 servings.

Fruity Rice Salad

1 c. cooked rice
1 (8½-oz.) can crushed pineapple,
    drained
1 c. miniature marshmallows
¼ c. sugar
1 medium apple, cored and cubed
¼ c. sliced red maraschino cherries
½ c. heavy cream, whipped

IN ADVANCE:

Combine cooked rice, pineapple, marshmallows and sugar in bowl; toss gently to mix well. Cover and refrigerate at least 3 hours. Fold in apples and cherries. Then fold in whipped cream. Chill at least 1 more hour before serving. Makes 6 servings.

Hard-Hat
Ice Cream Sundaes

1 (6-oz.) pkg. semisweet chocolate
    pieces
½ c. butter or regular margarine
1 qt. ice cream

IN ADVANCE:

Combine chocolate and butter in 1-qt. saucepan. Cook over low heat, stirring occasionally, until mixture is melted. Remove from heat and cool completely. Spoon over ice cream. (If not serving immediately, pour into bowl, cover and refrigerate until ready to serve.)

TO REHEAT:

Warm sauce in 1-qt. saucepan over low heat until fluid. Remove from heat and cool completely before spooning over ice cream. Makes 1¼ c. or 6 servings.

Marinated Beef Kabobs*

Green Salad

Birthday Cake

Vanilla Ice Cream*

Hot Fudge Sauce*

Peanut Butter Sauce*

Every day is someone's birthday—and what better way to celebrate than with an old-fashioned party topped off by homemade cake and ice cream. Children of all ages will enjoy a dish piled high with rich, creamy ice cream accompanied by a wedge of homemade cake. While the electric freezer is easier, many farm women tell us they prefer the old-fashioned crank method—they say that part of the joy of making ice cream is family participation. Everyone will want a turn at the crank in helping to prepare creamy Vanilla Ice Cream—it's well worth waiting for (and working for!). Serve assorted toppings with the ice cream; we've included recipes for a classic Hot Fudge Sauce and a caramel-colored Peanut Butter Sauce. While the ice cream ripens, grill the Chinese-inspired Marinated Beef Kabobs and serve them with a simple green salad.

Marinated Beef Kabobs

2½ lb. beef round steak (1" thick)
¾ c. cooking oil
⅓ c. soy sauce
⅓ c. lemon juice
2 tblsp. Worcestershire sauce
¼ c. finely chopped onion
3 tblsp. finely chopped fresh parsley
1 clove garlic, minced
¼ tsp. pepper
1 large green pepper, cut into 1½" chunks
12 white onions
3 small zucchini, cut into 1" thick slices
16 cherry tomatoes
1 (15¼-oz.) can pineapple chunks, drained

IN ADVANCE:
Cut beef into 1" cubes and place in bowl. Combine cooking oil, soy sauce, lemon juice, Worcestershire sauce, ¼ c. onion, parsley, garlic and pepper; mix well. Pour over beef cubes. Cover and refrigerate 24 to 48 hours.

TO GRILL:
Cook green pepper, 12 whole onions and sliced zucchini together in boiling water until tender-crisp. Drain well. Thread beef cubes, green pepper chunks, onions, zucchini slices, tomatoes and pineapple chunks alternately on 8 (12") skewers. Grill kabobs 4" from gray coals (medium heat), turning and basting often with marinade. Cook 12 to 15 minutes or to desired doneness. Makes 6 to 8 servings.

Vanilla Ice Cream

2 qt. heavy cream
2 c. milk
4 eggs, slightly beaten
½ c. sweetened condensed milk
1½ c. sugar

¼ tsp. salt
1 tsp. vanilla
crushed ice (about 20 lb.)
rock salt (about 2 lb.)

IN ADVANCE:

Heat 2 c. cream with milk in top of double boiler. Combine eggs, sweetened condensed milk, sugar and salt. Gradually blend in a little hot cream mixture; then slowly pour egg mixture back into double boiler. Cook 5 minutes over simmering water, stirring constantly, until it coats a spoon.

Set aside to cool. Stir in vanilla and remaining cream. Cover and refrigerate.

Scald freezer can and dasher. Pour chilled ice cream mixture into freezer can. Fill ⅔ to ¾ full to leave room for expansion. Fit can into freezer. (Follow manufacturer's directions if using an electric freezer.)

Adjust dasher and cover. Pack crushed ice and rock salt around can, using 8 parts ice to 1 part rock salt. (You will need about 20 lb. ice to freeze and ripen ice cream in a 1-gal. freezer.) Turn dasher slowly until ice melts enough to form a brine. Add more ice and salt, mixed in proper proportions, to maintain the ice level.

Turn handle fast and steadily until it is hard to turn. Then remove ice until its level is below the lid of the can; take lid off. Remove dasher.

To ripen the ice cream, plug the opening in the lid. Cover the can with several thicknesses of waxed paper or foil to make a tight fit for the lid. Put the lid on the can. Pack more of ice and salt (this time using 4 parts ice to 1 part rock salt) around can, filling freezer.

Cover freezer with a blanket, canvas or other heavy cloth, or with newspapers. Let ice cream ripen 2 hours. If you are allowing ice cream to ripen longer, pack in a mixture of 8 parts ice

to 1 part rock salt. (Or put the can in your home freezer to ripen.) Makes 1 gal.

Hot Fudge Sauce

4 (1-oz.) squares unsweetened chocolate
2 tblsp. butter or regular margarine
⅔ c. boiling water
1 c. sugar
¼ c. light corn syrup
2 tsp. vanilla

Combine chocolate and butter in 2-qt. saucepan. Cook over low heat until melted. Add boiling water and mix until well blended.

Stir in sugar and corn syrup. Cook over medium heat until mixture comes to a boil. Cover and simmer 3 minutes. Uncover and cook 4 minutes more, without stirring.

Remove from heat. Stir in vanilla. Serve immediately over ice cream. Makes 1⅔ c.

Peanut Butter Sauce

1¼ c. brown sugar, packed
⅔ c. light corn syrup
¼ c. butter or regular margarine
¼ tsp. salt
1 c. creamy peanut butter
⅔ c. milk
1 tsp. vanilla

Combine brown sugar, corn syrup, butter and salt in 2-qt. saucepan. Cook over medium heat until mixture comes to a boil. Cook 2 minutes. Remove from heat. Stir in peanut butter, milk and vanilla, mixing until smooth and creamy. Serve immediately over ice cream. Makes about 3 c.

STOP·AND·GO SUPPER

Pork and Pineapple on a Spit*

Make-ahead Popovers*

Vegetable-stuffed Zucchini*

Chilled Buttermilk Soup*

When everyone in the family is involved in an outdoor activity, it makes sense to plan a meal around the event. Pork and Pineapple on a Spit cooks practically attention-free. A mild ginger-flavored soy sauce compliments the pork and pineapple. Both the Vegetable-stuffed Zucchini and Make-ahead Popovers can be made early in the day and warmed before serving. For a simply elegant dessert, serve bowls of buttermilk soup with a dollop of whipped cream, strawberry preserves and a generous sprinkling of slivered almonds.

Pork and Pineapple on a Spit

2 tblsp. brown sugar, packed
2 tblsp. cornstarch
1 tsp. ground ginger
1 (13¾-oz.) can chicken broth
2 tblsp. soy sauce
1 tblsp. vinegar
1 fresh pineapple (about 3 lb.)
6 pork chops, 1″ thick

IN ADVANCE:

Combine brown sugar, cornstarch and ginger in a 2-qt. saucepan. Stir in chicken broth, soy sauce and vinegar. Cook over medium heat about 2 minutes, stirring constantly, until mixture boils and thickens. Remove from heat. Cover and refrigerate until ready to cook.

Cut off leafy end of pineapple and cut into 7 slices. Cover and refrigerate.

TO GRILL:

Heat sauce in a 2-qt. saucepan over medium heat. Slash fat on pork chops at frequent intervals. Starting with a pineapple slice, alternately thread pork chops and pineapple slices onto a spit, piercing each one at the center. Set spit forks into ends. Holding spit at both ends, turn. If one side drops downward, reposition weight so it is balanced. Tighten forks.

Place on gas grill rotisserie, close lid and grill over gray coals (medium heat), basting often with sauce. Cook 1 hour or until pork chops are tender.

Meanwhile, heat remaining sauce over medium heat until hot and bubbly. Pass extra sauce with meat. Makes 6 servings.

Make-ahead Popovers

3 eggs
1½ c. sifted flour
1½ c. milk
¾ tsp. salt
1½ tblsp. cooking oil

IN ADVANCE:

Combine eggs, flour, milk and salt in bowl. Beat with an electric mixer at low speed 1½ minutes. Add oil. Beat ½ minute more. Pour into 8 well-greased (6-oz.) custard cups.

Bake in 450° oven 15 minutes.

Reduce oven temperature to 350°. Bake 35 minutes more. Slit tops with sharp knife to let steam escape. Turn off oven. Let popovers stand in oven 10 minutes. Remove from custard cups. Cool on rack.

Wrap in aluminum foil. Freeze up to 4 weeks. Makes 8 popovers.

TO REHEAT:

Warm foil-wrapped popovers on grill.

Vegetable-stuffed Zucchini

4 zucchini (about ½ lb. each)
1 c. water
½ tsp. salt
4 strips bacon
½ c. chopped onion
2 medium tomatoes, chopped
1 c. cooked whole-kernel corn
⅛ tsp. pepper
½ c. grated Parmesan cheese

IN ADVANCE:

Cut zucchini in half lengthwise. Place, cut side down, in 12″ skillet. Add water and salt. Cover and cook over high heat until water boils. Reduce heat to low and simmer 15 minutes, or until zucchini are tender. Drain zucchini and cool.

Cook bacon in same skillet over medium heat until crisp. Remove and drain on paper towels. Crumble bacon and set aside. Add onion to bacon drippings in skillet and cook over medium heat until tender. Stir in tomatoes, corn and pepper. Cook until mixture comes to a boil. Remove from heat and set aside.

Scoop out seeds and pulp from zucchini, leaving ¼″ thick shells. Spoon ¼ c. tomato mixture into each shell. Sprinkle with cheese. Wrap in heavy-duty foil and refrigerate until ready to cook.

TO GRILL:

Heat foil-wrapped zucchini 4″ from gray coals (medium heat) 25 minutes or until hot. Makes 8 servings.

Chilled Buttermilk Soup

⅓ c. sugar
2 egg yolks
1 qt. buttermilk
1 tsp. lemon juice
1 c. heavy cream, whipped
1 c. blanched, slivered almonds
strawberry preserves

IN ADVANCE:

Combine sugar and egg yolks in bowl. Beat about 5 minutes, using an electric mixer at high speed, until thick and lemon-colored. Gently stir in buttermilk and lemon juice. Cover and refrigerate at least 3 hours before serving.

TO SERVE:

Top with whipped cream, almonds and strawberry preserves. Makes 1 qt. or 6 servings.

Lamb Kabobs*

Spinach Salad
with Hot Bacon Dressing*

Blueberry Grunt*

Tangerine-Apple Nectar*

Many outdoor cooks pick one good menu that suits their taste and stick with it. But outdoor cooking and eating can be an adventure if you experiment with new recipes and a variety of ingredients. Tender chunks of seasoned lamb served in crusty French bread warmed on the grill is pure sandwichery. The spinach salad is a wonderful concoction of spinach, water chestnuts, mushrooms, hard-cooked eggs and Cheddar cheese tossed with a hot bacon dressing. Blueberry Grunt, a New England adaptation of a basic Indian dish, features dumplings that are dropped into a simmering fruit sauce. An Illinois farm woman finds it an ideal campfire dessert; she mixes up the dry ingredients at home and assembles everything at the site.

Lamb Kabobs

2 lb. boneless lamb, cut into 1" cubes
1 c. chopped onion
⅔ c. cooking oil
⅓ c. cider vinegar
3 tblsp. lemon juice
2 tsp. dried parsley flakes
2 cloves garlic, minced
1 tsp. dried oregano leaves
1 tsp. salt
¼ tsp. pepper
1 (24") loaf French bread, cut into
   4" lengths

IN ADVANCE:
Combine all ingredients except bread in glass bowl; mix well. Cover and refrigerate overnight.
TO GRILL:
Thread lamb cubes on 6 skewers. Grill kabobs 4" from gray coals (medium heat), turning and basting often with marinade. Cook 15 to 20 minutes or to desired doneness.
To serve, split each length of French bread and fill with lamb. Makes 6 servings.

Spinach Salad with Hot Bacon Dressing

12 c. fresh spinach
1 c. fresh or canned (drained) bean
   sprouts
1 (8-oz.) can water chestnuts, drained and
   sliced
1 c. sliced fresh mushrooms
½ c. shredded Cheddar cheese
3 hard-cooked eggs, sliced
¼ c. cooking oil
¼ c. ketchup
¼ c. vinegar
¼ c. finely chopped onion

2 tblsp. barbecue sauce
2 tblsp. sugar
1 tblsp. steak sauce
1 tblsp. Worcestershire sauce
¼ tsp. Tabasco sauce
6 strips bacon, diced

IN ADVANCE:

In a large salad bowl, tear spinach into bite-size pieces. Add bean sprouts,
water chestnuts, mushrooms, cheese
and eggs. Cover and refrigerate.

Combine oil, ketchup, vinegar, onion,
barbecue sauce, sugar, steak sauce,
Worcestershire sauce and Tabasco sauce
in glass jar. Cover and shake to blend.
Refrigerate.

TO COOK:

Cook bacon in skillet until crisp.
Remove and drain on paper towels.
Pour off all but 2 tblsp. bacon
drippings. Stir in dressing mixture.
Cook over medium heat until mixture
simmers.

Add bacon to salad. Pour dressing
over salad. Toss lightly, but well. Makes
6 servings.

Blueberry Grunt

1 pt. fresh blueberries
1 c. water
½ c. sugar
1½ c. sifted flour
2 tsp. baking powder
¼ tsp. ground nutmeg
⅛ tsp. salt
¾ c. milk
2 tsp. grated orange rind

TO GRILL:

Combine blueberries, water and sugar
in a 10″ skillet. Cook 4″ from gray
coals (medium heat) until mixture
comes to a boil. Reduce heat to low and

simmer 5 minutes.

Meanwhile, sift together flour, baking
powder, nutmeg and salt into bowl.
Add milk and orange rind, stirring just
enough to moisten. Drop mixture by
spoonfuls on top of simmering blueberry mixture.

Cover and simmer 10 to 15 minutes
more or until dumplings are puffy and
wooden pick inserted in center comes
out clean. Serve immediately. Makes
6 servings.

Tangerine-Apple Nectar

1 (6-oz.) can frozen tangerine juice
    concentrate, thawed
3 c. apple cider or juice
1 c. cranberry juice
⅓ c. lime juice
2 c. water

IN ADVANCE:

Combine all ingredients; mix well.
Refrigerate.

TO SERVE:

Pour over ice cubes in glasses. Makes
6 (9-oz.) servings.

COMMUNITY COOKOUT

Barbecued Chicken Wings*

Pork with Peppery Peanut Dip*

Surprise Pizza Rolls*

Fresh Sliced Pineapple   Green Grapes

Cheddar Cheese with Rye Crackers

Lime Slush Punch*

Make your next barbecue a cooperative event with several families joining together, each one being responsible for bringing a different dish. Let a novice cook bring the ingredients for Barbecued Chicken Wings; each of these appetizers is bathed in a simple barbecue sauce and grilled to a crunchy goodness. Pork with Peppery Peanut Dip is a tasty and unusual main dish of pork cubes that are marinated, skewered and grilled, then offered with individual dishes of thick and peppery peanut sauce for dipping. Break open a Surprise Pizza Roll and you'll find a pepperoni-and-cheese center. The beverage is a wonderful icy punch that comes from the freezer a few hours before serving.

Barbecued Chicken Wings

¾ c. chili sauce
½ c. cola-flavored soda
½ tsp. onion salt
3 lb. chicken wings (about 16)

IN ADVANCE:

Combine chili sauce, soda and onion salt in bowl. Cover and refrigerate.

Cut off wing tips and reserve for soup, if you wish. Slicing through the joint, cut each wing in half. Cover and refrigerate.

TO GRILL:

Cook chicken 4″ from gray coals (medium heat), turning often with tongs. Cook 20 minutes.

Remove chicken from grill. Dip chicken in sauce and return to grill. Cook 10 minutes more, turning often, until well-glazed. Makes about 32 appetizers.

Pork with Peppery Peanut Dip

4 lb. boneless lean pork, cut into 1″ cubes
1 c. orange juice
½ c. cooking oil
¼ c. orange-flavored liqueur
2 tblsp. Worcestershire sauce
1 tsp. pepper
4 cloves garlic, crushed
Peppery Peanut Dip (recipe follows)

IN ADVANCE:

Combine pork, orange juice, cooking oil, orange liqueur, Worcestershire sauce, pepper and garlic in glass bowl. Cover and refrigerate overnight.

TO GRILL:

Thread pork cubes on skewers. Grill kabobs 4″ from gray coals (medium heat), turning often. Cook 30 minutes or until no longer pink in centers.

Meanwhile, prepare Peppery Peanut Dip. When done, serve pork immediately with dip. Makes 12 servings.

PEPPERY PEANUT DIP: Heat 1½ c. orange juice in 2-qt. saucepan over medium heat until hot. Remove from heat. Add 2 c. peanut butter, stirring until melted and well blended. Add 2 tsp. Worcestershire sauce, ½ tsp. Tabasco sauce and ½ tsp. pepper; mix well. Makes 3 c.

Surprise Pizza Rolls

1 (13¾-oz.) pkg. hot roll mix
¾ c. very warm water (105° to 115°)
1 egg
1 tblsp. butter or regular margarine
½ c. chopped onion
1 clove garlic, minced
1 (6-oz.) can tomato paste
1 c. shredded mozzarella cheese
¼ c. grated Parmesan cheese
1 tsp. dried oregano leaves
3 oz. pepperoni, thinly sliced
1 egg yolk
2 tsp. water
sesame seeds

IN ADVANCE:

Prepare hot roll mix according to package directions, using ¾ c. warm water and egg. Cover; let rise in warm place until doubled, about 45 minutes.

Meanwhile, melt butter in 7″ skillet over medium heat. Add onion and garlic, and sauté until tender. Remove from heat. Stir in tomato paste, mozzarella cheese, Parmesan cheese and oregano, mixing well. Set aside.

Punch down dough. Turn out on floured surface. Knead until smooth, about 2 minutes.

Divide dough into 24 sections. Roll out each section to a 4″ round. Divide pepperoni among rounds. Top each

with a rounded teaspoonful of tomato mixture. Bring all edges together over filling and pinch to seal. Place, seam side down, in greased 2½″ muffin-pan cups. Cover; let rise until almost doubled, about 30 minutes.

Beat together egg yolk and 2 tsp. water. Brush over rolls and sprinkle with sesame seeds.

Bake in 375° oven 12 minutes or until golden brown. Serve immediately; or cool completely, wrap in foil and refrigerate until ready to serve. Makes 24 rolls.

TO REHEAT:

Warm foil-wrapped rolls on grill.

Lime Slush Punch

1 (6-oz.) pkg. lime-flavored gelatin
2 c. boiling water
1 (16-oz.) can frozen orange juice concentrate
6 c. water
1 (46-oz.) can pineapple juice
1 qt. ginger ale, chilled
1 qt. club soda, chilled

IN ADVANCE:

Combine gelatin and 2 c. boiling water in 5-qt. bowl, stirring until gelatin is completely dissolved. Add orange juice concentrate, stirring until completely thawed. Add 6 c. water and pineapple juice. Mix well.

Pour into 5-qt. plastic bowl or 5 (1 qt.) plastic containers. Cover and freeze at least several hours. Mixture may be frozen up to 3 weeks before serving.

TO SERVE:

Remove frozen juice mixture from freezer and refrigerate 2 to 3 hours to thaw. Place in punch bowl and break up into pieces, using a spoon.

Add ginger ale and club soda. Mix lightly, but well. Makes 6 qt., or about 48 (4-oz.) servings.

Souper Gazpacho*

Taco Salad*

Mexican Chocolate Cake*

Sangria*

Good food is the best way to welcome friends in any language. *Souper Gazpacho*—a chilled, garlic-scented soup—is quickly made by whirling lots of fresh vegetables in a blender together with canned tomato soup. Main-dish *Taco Salad* features a mild chili-flavored ground beef mixture with a thick sour cream dressing. *Mexican Chocolate Cake* is really a North American dessert originally made in ranch kitchens with sour milk; these days it's usually made with buttermilk. Our homemade *Sangria* is a fruity wine punch.

Souper Gazpacho

1 c. chopped tomato
1 c. chopped green pepper
1 c. chopped, pared cucumber
½ c. chopped onion
1 clove garlic, minced
3 c. tomato juice
1 (10¾-oz.) can condensed tomato soup
1 c. water
¼ c. vinegar
2 tblsp. cooking oil
2 slices white bread, broken up
4 drops Tabasco sauce
assorted chopped vegetables

IN ADVANCE:
Place half of the tomato, green pepper, cucumber, onion, garlic, tomato juice, tomato soup, water, vinegar, oil, bread and Tabasco sauce in blender jar. Cover and blend until smooth. Pour into large bowl. Repeat. Cover and refrigerate at least 3 hours before serving.
TO SERVE:
Garnish with assorted chopped vegetables. Makes 1¾ qt. or 6 servings.

Taco Salad

1 c. dairy sour cream
1 c. mayonnaise
1 (1-oz.) pkg. buttermilk
   ranch dressing mix
1 lb. ground chuck
1 (1⅛-oz.) pkg. taco seasoning mix
1 c. water
1 head iceberg lettuce, torn into bite-size
   pieces
2 large tomatoes, cut into wedges
1½ c. shredded Cheddar cheese
1 c. sliced celery

½ of 1 (9-oz.) bag taco-flavored tortilla
chips, coarsely crushed
½ c. sliced black olives

IN ADVANCE:
Combine sour cream, mayonnaise
and dressing mix in bowl. Mix well.
Cover and refrigerate at least 30
minutes.

TO COOK:
Cook ground chuck in 10″ skillet over
medium heat 5 minutes or until browned. Drain fat from skillet.

Stir in taco seasoning mix and water.
Cook until mixture comes to a boil.
Reduce heat to low. Simmer 15 min-
utes. Remove from heat.

Arrange lettuce, tomatoes, cheese,
celery, tortilla chips and olives in bowl.
Add meat mixture and toss lightly to
mix well.

Serve with chilled dressing. Makes
6 servings.

Mexican Chocolate Cake

2 c. sifted flour
2 c. sugar
1 tsp. baking soda
1 tsp. salt
1½ tsp. ground cinnamon
½ tsp. baking powder
¾ c. water
¾ c. buttermilk
½ c. shortening
2 eggs
4 (1-oz.) squares unsweetened chocolate,
melted and cooled
1 tsp. vanilla
Chocolate Frosting (recipe follows)

IN ADVANCE:
Sift together flour, sugar, baking
soda, salt, cinnamon and baking
powder into large mixing bowl. Add

water, buttermilk, shortening, eggs,
melted chocolate and vanilla. Beat 30
seconds, using an electric mixer at low
speed, scraping sides and bottom of
bowl constantly. Beat at high speed
3 minutes, scraping bowl occasionally.
Spread batter evenly in greased and
floured 13x9x2″ baking pan.

Bake in 350° oven 40 to 45 minutes
or until cake tester or wooden pick inserted in center comes out clean.

Cool cake in pan on rack. Spread
cooled cake with Chocolate Frosting.
Makes 12 servings.

CHOCOLATE FROSTING: Combine
½ c. butter or regular margarine,
2 (1-oz.) squares unsweetened chocolate
and ¼ c. milk in 2-qt. saucepan. Cook
over low heat, stirring occasionally,
until tiny bubbles form around edge of
pan and chocolate melts. Remove from
heat. Add 1 (1-lb.) pkg. confectioners'
sugar (sifted) and 1 tsp. vanilla. Beat
until frosting reaches spreading
consistency, using an electric mixer at
low speed. Stir in ½ c. chopped pecans.
Add 1 to 2 tblsp. milk if necessary to
bring frosting to spreading consistency.

Sangria

1 (4/5-qt.) bottle dry red wine
1 orange, thinly sliced
1 lemon, thinly sliced
½ c. sugar
1 (28-oz.) bottle club soda

IN ADVANCE:
Combine wine, orange, lemon and
sugar in pitcher; stir well. Let stand at
room temperature about 1 hour.

TO SERVE:
Add club soda to wine mixture and
serve over ice. Makes 1½ qt. or
6 (8-oz.) servings.

Watermelon Fruit Basket*

Hamburgers on Toasted Buns

Sour Cream Potato Salad*

Party Baked Alaska*

H*aving everything ready the moment the hamburgers are done is good time management—and it's a must when you cook for a crowd. With that in mind, we've put together this make-ahead menu. A Watermelon Fruit Basket makes a spectacular edible centerpiece for the picnic table. The whole team can enjoy this fresh fruit appetizer while the hamburgers are grilling and you're putting the finishing touches on the potato salad. For dessert, Party Baked Alaska will bring "oh's" and "ah's" when it arrives at the table.*

Watermelon Fruit Basket

1 large, long watermelon (about 26 lb.)
4 c. cantaloupe balls, chilled
4 c. honeydew balls, chilled
1 pt. fresh strawberries, hulled
  and chilled
2 to 3 c. chilled ginger ale

Place watermelon on its side. Using a sharp knife, lightly mark a 2″ wide strip along the top of the watermelon. (This strip will form the handle of the basket.) At a point where the handle would meet the rim of the basket (about one-third down the side of the watermelon) mark a line all the way around the watermelon to the opposite end handle. Repeat on other side.

Using the lines as a guide, cut through rind into pulp and make the necessary cuts to form a removable wedge on either side of the handle. Remove wedges and set aside.

Cut an even saw-tooth pattern about 1″ deep all around the edge of the melon. Remove seeds and scoop out melon. Scoop melon into bite-size balls (about 8 c.) or cut into bite-size pieces.

Combine watermelon balls, cantaloupe balls, honeydew melon balls and strawberries. Toss lightly to mix well.

Return fruit mixture to watermelon basket. Slowly pour ginger ale over fruit. Makes 24 (6-oz.) servings.

Sour Cream Potato Salad

4 lb. new potatoes
¾ tsp. salt
¾ c. bottled Italian salad dressing
6 hard-cooked eggs
1 c. thinly sliced celery

1 c. sliced green onions
2¼ c. mayonnaise
¾ c. dairy sour cream
1 tblsp. prepared mustard
1 tsp. salt
1 tsp. prepared horseradish
½ tsp. celery seeds
¼ tsp. pepper
1 c. chopped pared cucumber
2 tblsp. sliced green onion tops

IN ADVANCE:

Cook potatoes in water with ¾ tsp. salt in Dutch oven 30 minutes or until tender. Drain; cool 10 minutes.

Peel potatoes and slice into bowl. Pour Italian dressing over potatoes. Cover and refrigerate at least 2 hours.

Remove egg yolks from egg whites; set aside. Chop egg whites. Add egg whites, celery and 1 c. green onions to potatoes. Set aside. Press egg yolks through sieve, reserving 3 tblsp. for garnish. Combine remaining egg yolks, mayonnaise, sour cream, mustard, salt, horseradish, celery seeds and pepper in bowl. Pour mayonnaise mixture over potatoes. Toss lightly to mix well.

Cover and refrigerate at least 2 hours before serving.

TO SERVE:

Toss cucumbers with potato salad Garnish with remaining 3 tblsp. sieved egg yolk and 2 tblsp. green onion tops. Makes 24 (½-c.) servings.

Party Baked Alaska

1½ c. sifted flour
1 tsp. baking powder
½ tsp. salt
4 eggs
1 c. sugar

1 c. brown sugar, packed
1½ tsp. vanilla
4 (1-oz.) squares unsweetened chocolate, melted and cooled
⅔ c. cooking oil
3 tblsp. instant coffee powder
1 c. chopped walnuts
½ gal. block chocolate ice cream
Meringue (recipe follows)

IN ADVANCE:

Sift together flour, baking powder and salt in bowl; set aside.

Combine eggs, sugar, brown sugar and vanilla in mixing bowl. Beat 2 minutes, using an electric mixer at high speed. Beat in chocolate, oil and coffee powder. Stir in dry ingredients and walnuts, mixing well. Spread batter in greased and waxed paper-lined 15½x10½x1″ jelly roll pan.

Bake in 350° oven 25 minutes or until top springs back when lightly touched with finger. Cool in pan on rack 10 minutes. Remove brownie layer from pan and cool completely on rack.

Place brownie layer on foil-lined baking sheet. Cut ice cream into 1″ slices. Arrange ice cream slices on brownie layer, leaving ¾″ uncovered around the edges. Freeze 2 hours or until firm.

Prepare Meringue. Quickly spread Meringue over entire surface of frozen ice cream and brownie layer, right down to foil. Freeze up to 24 hours.

TO SERVE:

Bake in 500° oven 3 minutes or until lightly browned. Makes 24 servings.

MERINGUE: Combine 8 egg whites, 1 tsp. cream of tartar and 1 tsp. vanilla in mixing bowl. Beat until foamy, using an electric mixer at high speed. Gradually add 1 c. sugar, 1 tblsp. at a time, beating well after each addition. Continue beating until stiff, glossy peaks form when beaters are lifted.

A COMPLETE MEAL ON THE GRILL

Frank-and-Pineapple Kabobs*

Hobo Meat Loaves*

Flaky Baking Powder Biscuits*

Grill-baked Butterscotch Bars*

Y*ou can save energy and keep your kitchen cool in the summertime if you use your grill to cook a complete meal. Hobo Meat Loaves—made with ground beef, onion, bread crumbs and Cheddar cheese—are paired with succotash in foil packets and cooked on the grill. Serve them with Flaky Baking Powder Biscuits cooked in a skillet over the grill; for easy mixing at the cookout, you can cut the shortening into the dry ingredients before you leave home. For dessert, a Maryland farm woman who really knows how to get the most out of her grill suggests rich and chewy Grill-baked Butterscotch Bars.*

Frank-and-Pineapple Kabobs

4 frankfurters
1 (8-oz.) can sliced pineapple, drained
3 tblsp. currant jelly
1 tsp. prepared mustard

IN ADVANCE:
Cut each frankfurter and each slice of pineapple into 4 sections. Alternately thread pineapple and frankfurter sections on 16 (3″) wooden skewers. Cover and refrigerate.

TO GRILL:
Heat jelly in 1-qt. saucepan over low heat until melted and smooth. Stir in mustard. Remove from heat. Dip kabobs in melted mixture.

Grill kabobs 4″ from gray coals (medium heat), turning and basting often with glaze. Cook about 14 to 16 minutes.

Remove from heat and baste with any remaining glaze. Makes 16 kabobs or 8 servings.

Hobo Meat Loaves

2 lb. ground beef
1 c. shredded Cheddar cheese
¾ c. milk
½ c. chopped onion
½ c. soft bread crumbs
2 eggs
1 tsp. salt
¼ tsp. dry mustard
⅛ tsp. pepper
2 (10-oz.) pkg. frozen lima beans, thawed
2 (10-oz.) pkg. frozen corn, thawed
½ c. ketchup

Combine ground beef, cheese, milk, onion, bread crumbs, eggs, salt, dry mustard and pepper in a bowl. Mix lightly but well. Divide mixture into 8 equal portions. Shape each portion into a small loaf. Place each loaf on a 12″ length of heavy-duty foil and set aside.

Combine beans and corn in bowl. Toss lightly to mix well. Spoon equal amounts of vegetable mixture along both sides of each loaf. Spread 1 tblsp. ketchup over each loaf. Securely wrap each loaf into a loose packet and refrigerate.

TO GRILL:

Cook loaf packets 4″ from gray coals (medium heat), turning often with tongs. Grill 30 to 40 minutes or until done. Makes 8 servings.

Flaky Baking Powder Biscuits

2 c. sifted flour
4 tsp. baking powder
2 tsp. sugar
½ tsp. salt
½ tsp. cream of tartar
½ c. shortening
⅔ c. light cream

Sift together flour, baking powder, sugar, salt and cream of tartar in a bowl. Cut in shortening until coarse crumbs form, using a pastry blender.

Add cream, stirring just enough with a fork to make a soft dough that sticks together. Turn onto lightly floured surface and knead gently 10 times. Pat to ¾″ thickness. Cut with floured 2″ cutter and place in lightly greased 10″ skillet.

TO GRILL:

Cover and cook over low heat 15 minutes or until golden brown on the bottom. Turn biscuits over and cook, covered, 5 minutes. Uncover and cook 5 minutes more or until golden brown. Serve immediately. Makes 12 biscuits.

Grill-baked Butterscotch Bars

1 c. sifted flour
1 tsp. baking powder
¾ c. brown sugar, packed
¼ c. butter or regular margarine
½ c. butterscotch-flavored pieces
1 egg
½ tsp. vanilla
½ c. chopped walnuts

IN ADVANCE:

Using heavy-duty foil, construct a heat deflector (see p. 00).

TO COOK:

Place heat deflector on the grill. Preheat grill and reduce temperature to low.

Sift together flour and baking powder in bowl. Set aside.

Combine brown sugar and butter in 2-qt. saucepan. Cook over medium heat, stirring occasionally, until butter is melted and mixture begins to bubble. Remove from heat and stir in butterscotch. Mix until butterscoch is melted. Cool slightly.

Add egg and beat well. Blend in vanilla. Add dry ingredients and mix well. Stir in walnuts. Spread mixture in greased 8″ square baking pan. Place on heat deflector on grill.

Close lid and bake at low heat 20 minutes or until done. Cool in baking pan on rack. Cut into 2″ squares. Makes 16 squares.

Rolled Roast on a Spit*

Cheese-stuffed Potatoes*

Marinated Vegetables*

Russian Torte*

You can honor your partner and your corner with a late-night supper of rolled rib roast that cooks unattended on a spit while you do-si-do. Cheese-stuffed Potatoes are baked early in the day and stuffed with a bacon-and-cheese mixture. They can be put on the grill after the meat is done and reheated in minutes. Marinated Vegetables team a tangy mustard-based marinade with tender-crisp vegetables. It will keep refrigerated several days. After supper, promenade in with an unforgettable dessert—this elegant Russian Torte starts with a prepared angel food cake that you slice into layers and frost with fluffy coffee-flavored filling.

Rolled Roast on a Spit

⅓ c. ketchup
¾ c. dry red wine
½ c. salad oil
1 tblsp. Worcestershire sauce
1 tsp. dried rosemary leaves
1½ tsp. salt
¼ tsp. pepper
1 (3 to 5-lb.) boneless rolled rib beef roast

IN ADVANCE:
Combine all ingredients except roast in bowl. Mix well. Place roast in bowl, turning over to coat with marinade on all sides. Cover; refrigerate overnight.
TO GRILL:
Lift roast from marinade and drain briefly, reserving marinade. Run spit through center of roast. Set spit forks on ends and tighten. Insert a meat thermometer into the center of the thickest portion, being careful not to touch spit.

Place on gas grill rotisserie, close lid and grill over medium-low coals, basting often with marinade. Cook 1½ hours or until thermometer registers 135° for rare, or to desired doneness.

Let roast stand 20 minutes before slicing. Makes 6 servings plus leftovers.

Cheese-stuffed Potatoes

6 baking potatoes (3 lb.)
6 strips bacon
6 tblsp. butter or regular margarine
1 tsp. salt
⅛ tsp. pepper
1 c. milk
2 tblsp. finely chopped onion
1½ c. shredded Cheddar cheese

IN ADVANCE:
Prick potatoes several times with a fork. Using 6 (12″) lengths of heavy-duty foil, securely wrap each potato into a loose packet and grill 4″ from

gray coals (medium heat), turning often with tongs. (Or bake conventionally.) Cook 25 to 35 minutes or until potatoes are tender.

Meanwhile, cook bacon in 10″ skillet over medium heat 5 minutes or until crisp. Drain on paper towels. Crumble; set aside.

Cool cooked potatoes slightly. Slice off tops. Scoop out potatoes with spoon and place in mixing bowl, setting aside skins. Add butter, salt, pepper, milk, onion and 1 c. of the cheese. Beat until smooth, using an electric mixer at medium speed. Stir in bacon. Spoon mixture back into potato skins. Cover and refrigerate.

TO REHEAT:

Place each potato on a 12″ length of heavy-duty foil and wrap securely into a loose packet. Grill 4″ from gray coals (medium heat) 5 to 10 minutes or until hot, being careful not to overheat. Top with remaining cheese. Makes 6 servings.

Marinated Vegetables

2½ c. water
2¼ tsp. salt
1 lb. carrots, pared and diagonally sliced
1½ lb. head cauliflower, broken
    into flowerets
1 lb. fresh green beans, cut
    into 1½″ pieces
1½ c. salad oil
1 c. white wine vinegar
1½ c. salad oil
1 c. white wine vinegar
1½ tsp. salt
¾ tsp. dry mustard
¼ tsp. pepper

IN ADVANCE:

Heat water and salt in 4-qt. Dutch oven over high heat until it comes to a boil. Add carrots, cauliflower and green beans. Return water to a boil. Reduce

heat and drain. Plunge drained vegetables into a bowl of iced water. Set aside.

Combine oil, vinegar, salt, mustard and pepper in bowl. Mix well. Set aside. Drain vegetables and place with cherry tomatoes and green onions in 13x9x2″ (3-qt.) glass baking dish. Pour marinade over vegetables. Toss lightly to mix well.

Cover and refrigerate overnight. Makes 6 servings plus leftovers.

Russian Torte

1 env. unflavored gelatin
¼ c. cold water
2 tblsp. instant coffee powder
1 c. sifted confectioners' sugar
⅛ tsp. salt
8 egg yolks
1 tsp. vanilla
2 c. heavy cream, whipped
1 (10″) angel food cake
toasted sliced almonds

IN ADVANCE:

Combine gelatin and cold water in 1-qt. saucepan. Cook over low heat until gelatin is completely dissolved. Remove from heat. Stir in coffee powder, confectioners' sugar and salt; cool to room temperature.

Beat egg yolks in mixing bowl until thick and lemon-colored, using an electric mixer at high speed, about 5 minutes. Beat in gelatin mixture. Fold egg yolk mixture and vanilla into whipped cream.

Slice angel food cake into 3 horizontal layers. Frost between layers with equal amounts of cream mixture. Then frost sides and top of cake. Decorate top with toasted almonds.

Refrigerate until ready to serve. Makes 12 servings.

Marinated Chuck Roast*

Cheesy Potato Casserole*

Herbed Cherry Tomatoes*

Grilled Banana Boats*

All cooks like to hear compliments about the meals they prepare, even when they've taken a shortcut route to a good meal. Sure to win praise at your next barbecue is Marinated Chuck Roast with a bourbon-based marinade that gives it the flavor of an expensive cut of beef. Cheesy Potato Casserole is an easy-does-it accompaniment, and Herbed Cherry Tomatoes will brighten your table. A fresh fruit dessert of grilled bananas—rich and gooey with melted marshmallows and chocolate—tastes just like a banana split.

Marinated Chuck Roast

¼ c. bourbon
¼ c. soy sauce
¼ c. brown sugar, packed
1 tblsp. Worcestershire sauce
1 tsp. lemon juice
1 (3½-lb.) beef chuck roast

IN ADVANCE:
Combine all ingredients except roast in glass bowl. Mix well. Add roast, turning to coat all sides. Cover and refrigerate 24 hours, turning occasionally.
TO GRILL:
Cook roast 4″ from gray coals (medium heat), turning and basting with marinade every 15 minutes. Cook 1 hour or to desired doneness. Makes 8 servings.

Cheesy Potato Casserole

1 (11-oz.) can condensed Cheddar
  cheese soup
1 (10¾-oz.) can condensed cream
  of mushroom soup
¼ c. water
2 tblsp. soy sauce
3 lb. all-purpose potatoes, pared and cut
  into ¾″ cubes
4 medium onions, quartered
2 c. sliced, celery
1 c. sliced, pared carrots
1 (8-oz.) can sliced water chestnuts,
  drained

IN ADVANCE:
  Combine cheese soup, mushroom
soup, water and soy sauce in bowl. Mix
well. Cover and refrigerate.
TO GRILL:
  Combine potatoes, onions, celery,
carrots and water chestnuts on a 36″
length of heavy-duty foil. Mix lightly,
but well. Pour soup mixture evenly over
vegetables and securely wrap mixture
into a loose packet. Grill packet 4″
from gray coals (medium heat) 1 hour
or until tender. Makes 8 servings.

Herbed Cherry Tomatoes

2 pt. cherry tomatoes
6 tblsp. butter or regular margarine
2 cloves garlic, minced
½ tsp. dried oregano leaves

IN ADVANCE:
  Wash and stem tomatoes. Melt butter
in skillet over medium heat. Add garlic
and oregano and sauté 2 minutes. Cut a
24″ length of heavy-duty foil and arrange tomatoes on top. Pour butter
mixture over tomatoes. Securely wrap
tomatoes into a loose packet and
refrigerate.
TO GRILL:
  Cook packet 6″ from gray coals
(medium heat) 8 to 10 minutes, shifting
packet occasionally. Makes 8 servings.

Grilled Banana Boats

8 firm bananas
¾ c. miniature marshmallows
⅓ c. semisweet chocolate pieces

IN ADVANCE:
  Cut each unpeeled banana almost in
half lengthwise. Stuff each banana with
an equal amount of marshmallows and
chocolate. Place each banana on a 10″
length of heavy-duty foil. Securely wrap
each banana into a loose packet and
refrigerate.
TO GRILL:
  Cook packets, cut side up, 4″ from
gray coals (medium heat). Cook 30 to
35 minutes or until marshmallows and
chocolate are melted. Serve in packets
and eat with spoons. Makes 8 servings.

Miniature Quiches*

Curried Sour Cream Dip
with Fresh Vegetables*

Fresh Fruit Compote*

Invite friends to stop by before a concert or after the theater to share a light and elegant repast—served outdoors, of course, beneath a star-studded sky. Miniature Quiches are a mouth-watering blend of creamy custard, bacon bits, onion and cheese encircled by flaky crusts. Arrange a colorful platter of raw vegetables around a crock of Curried Sour Cream Dip. An Illinois farm woman makes Fresh Fruit Compote year-round; in winter she substitutes canned fruits for fresh. This festive-looking dessert also can travel to potluck suppers in a large brandy snifter, to double as a center-piece.

Miniature Quiches

Basic Pastry (recipe follows)
8 strips bacon, diced
½ c. chopped onion
1½ c. shredded Swiss cheese
¼ c. grated Parmesan cheese
4 eggs
1¾ c. milk
1 tsp. Worcestershire sauce
3 drops Tabasco sauce
ground nutmeg

IN ADVANCE:
Prepare Basic Pastry and divide pastry in half. Roll out each half on a floured surface to ⅛" thickness. Cut 12 rounds from each half, using floured 3½" cookie cutter with scalloped edge. Reroll pastry as needed. Line 3" muffin-pan cups with rounds. Set aside.

Sauté bacon and onion in 10" skillet until browned. Drain on paper towels. Combine bacon mixture, Swiss cheese and Parmesan cheese in bowl. Place 1 rounded tblsp. cheese mixture in each prepared shell.

Combine eggs, milk, Worcestershire sauce and Tabasco sauce in bowl. Beat until blended, using a rotary beater. Spoon 2 tblsp. egg mixture into each cheese-filled shell. Sprinkle with nutmeg.

Bake in 425° oven 20 minutes or until set. Cool in pans on racks 5 minutes. Remove from pans. Cool completely, wrap in foil and refrigerate (or serve immediately). Makes 24 little quiches.

TO REHEAT:
Place foil-wrapped quiches on baking sheets and bake in 350° oven 10 minutes or until hot.

BASIC PASTRY: Combine 2 c. sifted flour and 1 tsp. salt in bowl. Cut in ⅔ c. shortening until coarse crumbs form, using a pastry blender. Sprinkle 4 to 5 tblsp. iced water over crumb mixture a little at a time, tossing with a fork until dough forms. Press dough firmly into a ball.

Curried Sour Cream Dip with Fresh Vegetables

2 c. dairy sour cream
2 tblsp. chopped fresh parsley
1 tblsp. finely chopped green onion
½ tsp. celery salt
¼ tsp. curry powder
vegetable dippers: carrot sticks, zucchini
  slices, broccoli flowerets and
  cauliflower flowerets

IN ADVANCE:
  Combine all ingredients except vegetable dippers in bowl. Mix well. Cover and refrigerate.
  Meanwhile, wash and prepare vegetable dippers, place in plastic bags and refrigerate.
TO SERVE:
  Arrange vegetables on platter. Serve with dip. Makes 2 c.

Fresh Fruit Compote

2 (3-oz.) pkg. cream cheese, softened
½ c. finely chopped pecans
2 c. fresh pitted Bing cherry halves
2 c. quartered, pitted plums
Maraschino Cherry Sauce
  (recipe follows)
2 bananas
2 tblsp. lemon juice
1 pt. red raspberries

IN ADVANCE:
  Cut each package of cream cheese into 9 cubes. Shape each cube into a ball and roll in pecans. Refrigerate.
  Combine cherries and plums in large bowl. Refrigerate.
TO SERVE:
  Slice bananas and sprinkle with lemon juice. Gently stir bananas, raspberries and Marachino Cherry Sauce into cherry mixture. Spoon mixture into a large glass bowl. Top with cream cheese balls. Makes 12 servings.
MARASCHINO CHERRY SAUCE:
Combine ¾ c. sugar and 1 tblsp. cornstarch in 2-qt. saucepan. Stir in ¼ c. light corn syrup, ¼ c. maraschino cherry juice, ¼ c. orange juice and ½ c. water. Cook over medium heat, stirring constantly, until mixture comes to a boil. Cook 3 minutes more, or until mixture is thick and slightly syrupy. Remove from heat. Crush 6 chopped maraschino cherries with a fork (skins will pop off). Remove skins and discard. Stir crushed cherries and 3 drops red food coloring into juice mixture. Refrigerate in covered container. Makes 1¼ c.

Autumn Gatherings

For many farm families, harvest time is a hectic period when work continues 'round the clock and the midday meal is likely to be served from the back of a pickup or station wagon at the end of a field of corn, or wherever the combine happens to be. For those with more relaxed schedules, autumn is the time for weekend hikes amid brilliant fall foliage, informal feasting at football games and other casual outdoor get-togethers.

Whether it's part of a workday or the center of a party, a tailgate buffet can be special with a little planning. For brisk days, you'll find recipes for Easy Salmon Chowder (p. 112), Chunky Lentil Soup (p. 132), Parslied Chicken Chowder (p. 118), and a spicy Texican Chili made with plenty of beef (p. 122).

Use your grill to prepare an Octoberfest menu of Bratwurst and Onions served in homemade buns (p. 120), or to cook a pork roast marinated with honey, garlic and soy sauce (p. 116). Plan to cook an entire meal over the coals using our Back-to-School Barbecue menu (p. 110) featuring individual-sized beef loaves and a packet of fresh green beans topped with bay leaves and butter.

Main courses that are meant to be prepared in advance and toted to your outdoor table include an Iowa farm woman's recipe for Main-Dish Potato Salad (p. 114), a cool and delicious meal in a bowl featuring cubed ham and potatoes in a creamy blend of cottage cheese and sour cream. Barbecued Chicken in a Bag (p. 104) cooks in the oven and travels to your picnic site right in its own cooking bag, and Two-Step Bean Cassoulet (p. 106) is a hearty casserole of pork and beans that requires little preparation.

In this chapter you'll also find scrumptious desserts from farm kitchens across the country. Two desserts that cook over the grill are Apples Alfresco (p. 121) and Cinnamon Pears (p. 111)—both made with fresh fruit. Weeks in advance of an impromptu picnic, you can freeze orange-iced Apricot Bars (p. 119) or an ultra-creamy Frosty Strawberry Torte (p. 117). For chocolate fans, there are make-ahead recipes for Chocolate Pound Cake (p. 133), Peanut Butter Brownies (p. 129), and a young Iowa farm woman's light and moist chocolate cake (p. 127).

Holiday and company menus are here, too. Our peppery recipe for grilled leg of lamb (p. 109) serves 12; the menu also features Stuffed Cherry Tomatoes, fresh butternut squash and a loaf of buttery Herbed French Bread. To add a gourmet touch to chicken drumsticks, marinate them with a subtle blend of lemon and rosemary (p. 130); serve them with homemade Sweet Potato Salad and treat yourself to a light, creamy dessert of Raspberry-Vanilla Cloud (p. 131).

And before autumn is over, consider planning a truly American picnic like the once-a-year menu suggested on page 124: an outdoor feast of turkey with all the trimmings. Our Pilgrims' Picnic features Cranberry-Orange Salad, Herbed Split Turkey that cooks to succulent tenderness in only 1½ hours alongside foil-wrapped sweet potatoes, and an extra-creamy Pumpkin Cheese Pie.

Fruit-Nut Mix*

Stuffed Franks*

Sweet-and-Sour Baked Beans*

Cabbage Slaw

Lazy Daisy Cake*

Next time you're exploring new paths, take along bags of Fruit-Nut Mix to provide wholesome munchies by the handful. You wouldn't want to backpack the other dishes in this menu into the wilderness, but they'll travel to your picnic site in a camper. The Stuffed Franks are a North Carolina farm woman's recipe for turning frankfurters that are ho-hum ordinary into extraordinary. They're split and stuffed with a mildly seasoned cracker crumb mixture that turns to a golden puff over the heat of the grill. If you simmer the Sweet-and-Sour Baked Beans at home in your slow cooker, they'll keep warm until you lift the lid at the picnic table. We think the Lazy Daisy Cake tastes best served warm, so bake it ahead of time and warm it over the grill.

Fruit-Nut Mix

1 lb. dry-roasted unsalted peanuts (3 c.)
1 (15-oz.) box raisins
½ lb. pitted dates, cut up (1¼ c.)
¼ lb. unroasted cashew pieces (1 c.)
¼ lb. walnut pieces (1 c.)
1 (3½-oz.) can flaked coconut
3 oz. dried apricots, cut in half (½ c.)

IN ADVANCE:
Combine all ingredients in large bowl; toss to mix. Place in airtight container or plastic bags and store in refrigerator up to six months. Makes about 3¼ lb. or 11 c.

Stuffed Franks

2 c. cracker crumbs
½ c. finely chopped celery
⅓ c. evaporated milk
¼ c. finely chopped onion
¼ c. chopped pimiento
¼ c. chopped fresh parsley
¼ c. butter or regular margarine, melted
¼ tsp. pepper
12 frankfurters
¾ c. ketchup

IN ADVANCE:
Combine cracker crumbs, celery, milk, onion, pimiento, parsley, butter and pepper in bowl. Mix lightly, but well. Set aside.

Place frankfurters in pairs on 6 (12") lengths of heavy-duty foil. Split frankfurters lengthwise almost halfway through and stuff each with ¼ c. crumb mixture. Spoon ketchup evenly over each frankfurter. Securely wrap each portion into a loose packet and refrigerate.
TO GRILL:
Cook frankfurter packets 6" from red-gray coals (high heat). Grill 15 minutes (do not turn packets). Makes 6 servings.

Clockwise from top: Marathon Cookies,
Chunky Chicken Salad on Rye, and
Frozen Cuke and Onion Relish (pp. 38-39).

From top: Peanut Butter Brownies, Beef 'n' Egg Loaves, Bacon-Cheese Macaroni, and Six-Vegetable Salad (pp. 128-129).

Ginger-glazed Spareribs (p. 70).

Kansas-style Beef Tacos (p. 62).

Sweet-and-Sour Baked Beans

1 lb. dried navy beans
6 c. water
8 strips bacon, cut into 1″ pieces
1 c. chopped onion
1 c. chopped celery
1 clove garlic, minced
1 (15-oz.) can tomato sauce
½ c. chili sauce
¼ c. molasses
¼ c. brown sugar, packed
1 tsp. salt
¼ tsp. pepper
⅛ tsp. Tabasco sauce
2 (8-oz.) cans pineapple chunks, drained and cut into halves
½ c. chopped sweet pickles
¼ c. sliced pimiento-stuffed olives

IN ADVANCE:

Wash navy beans thoroughly and place in 3½-qt. slow cooker. Add water and soak overnight.

The next day, cover slow cooker and cook on high setting 3 hours or until tender. Drain beans and set aside.

Fry bacon in 10″ skillet over medium heat until crisp. Remove bacon and drain on paper towels.

Sauté onion, celery and garlic in bacon drippings until tender. Stir in tomato sauce, chili sauce, molasses, brown sugar, salt, pepper and Tabasco sauce. Cook over high heat until mixture comes to a boil. Remove from heat.

Combine beans, bacon, tomato sauce mixture, pineapple, pickles and olives in slow cooker; mix well.

Cover and cook on high setting 3½ to 4½ hours. Makes 6 servings.

Lazy Daisy Cake

1 c. sifted flour
1 tsp. baking powder
¼ tsp. salt
2 tblsp. butter or regular margarine
½ c. milk
2 eggs
1 c. sugar
1 tsp. vanilla
Coconut-Pecan Topping (recipe follows)

IN ADVANCE:

Sift together flour, baking powder and salt; set aside.

Heat butter and milk over low heat until butter melts. Keep milk mixture warm.

Beat together eggs and sugar in bowl 2 minutes, using an electric mixer at medium speed. Gradually beat in dry ingredients and vanilla, using an electric mixer at low speed. Add hot milk mixture to egg mixture, beating until blended. Pour into greased 9″ square baking pan.

Bake in 375° oven 20 minutes, or until top springs back when touched lightly with finger. Cool in pan on rack 10 minutes. Meanwhile, prepare Coconut-Pecan Topping. Spread warm cake with Coconut-Pecan Topping. Place under broiler, 3″ from source of heat, until lightly browned and bubbly. Cool in pan on rack. Makes 9 servings.

COCONUT-PECAN TOPPING: Combine ½ c. butter or regular margarine, ¾ c. brown sugar (packed), 1 c. flaked coconut, ½ c. chopped pecans and 4 tblsp. light cream in small saucepan. Cook over medium heat until mixture comes to a boil. Remove from heat.

Barbecued Chicken in a Bag*

Corn on the Cob

Garden Salad*   Vinaigrette Dressing*

Banana Cake with Penuche Frosting*

More than one wary eyebrow was raised when an Iowa farm woman arrived at her 4-H club picnic toting a baking pan filled with a large bag. "I took the pan right from the oven and wrapped it in a terry dish towel," she explained. "When we got to the picnic, I slit open the bag and it was still good and hot." Her recipe for Barbecued Chicken in a Bag was a hit! Banana Cake with Penuche Frosting is another good traveler—it's iced and served right in the baking pan.

Barbecued Chicken in a Bag

¼ c. water
3 tblsp. ketchup
3 tblsp. brown sugar, packed
2 tblsp. cider vinegar
2 tblsp. Worcestershire sauce
2 tblsp. butter or regular margarine
1 tblsp. lemon juice
2 tsp. dry mustard
1 tsp. chili powder
1 tsp. paprika
⅓ c. flour
1 tsp. salt
¼ tsp. pepper
2 (3-lb.) broiler-fryers, cut up

IN ADVANCE:
Combine water, ketchup, brown sugar, vinegar, Worcestershire sauce, butter, lemon juice, mustard, chili powder and paprika in 2-qt. saucepan. Cook over medium heat until mixture comes to a boil. Remove from heat.

Combine flour, salt and pepper in large oven-browning bag. Add chicken and shake to coat well. Place in shallow roasting pan. Open bag and pour sauce over chicken. Secure bag loosely with twist tie and pierce top of bag 6 times with sharp knife.

Bake in 350° oven 1 hour or until tender.

TO SERVE:
Remove chicken from bag. Pour sauce into bowl and ladle off excess fat. Serve chicken with sauce. Makes 8 servings.

Garden Salad

3 c. bite-size pieces romaine lettuce
3 c. bite-size pieces fresh spinach
1 cucumber, sliced
½ lb. zucchini or summer squash, sliced
½ lb. fresh mushrooms, sliced

Combine ingredients in salad bowl. Toss lightly to mix well. Just before serving, toss lightly with Vinaigrette Dressing. Makes 8 servings.

Vinaigrette Dressing

⅔ c. salad oil
¼ c. white wine vinegar
2 cloves garlic, crushed
1 tsp. Italian herb seasoning
½ tsp. salt
⅛ tsp. pepper

IN ADVANCE:
Combine ingredients in bowl. Mix well. Cover and refrigerate. Makes about 1 c.

Banana Cake with Penuche Frosting

2¼ c. sifted cake flour
1¼ tsp. baking powder
1¼ tsp. baking soda
1 tsp. salt
2 tsp. vinegar
milk
⅔ c. shortening
1⅔ c. sugar
3 eggs
1¼ c. mashed ripe bananas (3 to 4 medium)
1 c. chopped walnuts
Penuche Frosting (recipe follows)

IN ADVANCE:
Sift together cake flour, baking powder, baking soda and salt; set aside.

Place vinegar in measuring cup. Add enough milk to make ⅔ c.; set aside.

Cream together shortening and sugar in mixing bowl until light and fluffy, using an electric mixer at medium speed. Add eggs one at a time, beating well after each addition.

Add dry ingredients alternately with milk mixture and bananas to creamed mixture, beating well after each addition, using an electric mixer at low speed. Stir in walnuts. Pour batter into greased 13x9x2" baking pan.

Bake in 350° oven 45 minutes or until cake tester or wooden pick inserted in center comes out clean. Cool in pan on rack.

Frost with Penuche Frosting. Makes 16 servings.

PENUCHE FROSTING: Heat ½ c. butter or regular margarine in 2-qt. saucepan over medium heat until bubbly but not browned.

Stir in 1 c. brown sugar (packed). Cook, stirring constantly, until mixture comes to a boil. Reduce heat to low and cook, stirring constantly, 2 minutes more.

Stir in ¼ c. milk. Increase heat to medium and cook until mixture returns to a boil. Remove from heat and cool to lukewarm.

Stir in 2 c. sifted confectioners' sugar and beat with a wooden spoon until well blended and thick enough to spread.

If necessary, place pan in bowl of ice water and beat with a wooden spoon until frosting reaches spreading consistency. If frosting becomes too stiff, warm over low heat.

Two-Step Bean Cassoulet*

Lettuce Wedges

Mock Russian Dressing*

Snappy Cheddar Loaf*

Frosted Spice Squares*

No one should have to work on Labor Day, so let casual cookery make the day a real holiday. Two-Step Bean Cassoulet begins the night before; then it practically cooks itself in your slow cooker. Pack the cassoulet right in the slow cooker to keep it warm while you travel to your picnic site. Mock Russian Dressing, a quick recipe enriched with yogurt, makes crisp wedges of lettuce taste special. To save minutes at meal-time, spread a crusty loaf of French bread with a zingy cheese mixture early in the day and refrigerate; then heat it on the grill when it's time for dinner. The Frosted Spice Squares are soft, cake-like bar cookies with a good old-fashioned country flavor, and they bake in the oven in half an hour.

Two-Step Bean Cassoulet

1 lb. dried navy beans
6 c. water
12 strips bacon, diced
1 lb. boneless pork, cut into ½" cubes
1 c. finely chopped onion
2 cloves garlic, minced
1 bay leaf
¾ tsp. dried thyme leaves
½ tsp. salt
⅛ tsp. pepper

IN ADVANCE:

Wash navy beans thoroughly. Soak overnight in water in 3½-qt. slow cooker.

The next day, cover and cook the beans in the slow cooker (high setting) 3 hours or until tender. Drain beans, reserving 2 c. cooking liquid.

Meanwhile, fry bacon in 10″ skillet over medium heat 5 minutes or until crisp. Remove with slotted spoon and drain on paper towels. Brown pork cubes in pan drippings 5 minutes. Combine beans, bacon, pork, 2 c. reserved cooking liquid, onion, garlic, bay leaf, thyme, salt and pepper in slow cooker.

Cover and cook (low setting) 5 hours or until pork is tender. Makes 6 to 8 servings.

Mock Russian Dressing

1 c. mayonnaise-type salad dressing
1 (8-oz.) container plain yogurt
1 (8-oz.) can tomato sauce
¼ c. finely chopped onion
¼ c. finely chopped celery
¼ c. finely chopped green pepper

IN ADVANCE:
Combine all ingredients in bowl. Mix well.

Cover and refrigerate at least 2 hours before serving. Makes 3 c.

Snappy Cheddar Loaf

½ c. butter or regular margarine, softened
½ c. cold-pack Cheddar cheese food
1 tsp. Worcestershire sauce
⅛ tsp. Tabasco sauce
1 (20″) loaf French bread

IN ADVANCE:
Combine butter, cheese food, Worcestershire sauce and Tabasco sauce in bowl. Beat until well blended, using an electric mixer at medium speed. Set aside.

Cut French bread into 1″ slices. Spread slices with butter mixture. Reassemble slices to form a loaf on a 28″ length of heavy-duty foil. Securely wrap loaf into a loose packet and refrigerate.

TO GRILL:
Cook bread 4″ from gray coals (medium heat). Grill about 15 minutes, turning once, or until butter mixture is melted and bread is hot. Makes 1 loaf.

Frosted Spice Squares

1½ c. sifted flour
1½ tsp. baking powder
1 tsp. ground cinnamon
½ tsp. salt
¼ tsp. ground cloves
¼ tsp. baking soda
½ c. shortening
½ c. sugar
1 egg
½ c. molasses
½ c. water
Confectioners' Sugar Icing (recipe follows)

IN ADVANCE:
Sift together flour, baking powder, cinnamon, salt, cloves and baking soda; set aside.

Cream together shortening and sugar in mixing bowl until light and fluffy, using an electric mixer at medium speed. Add egg, beating well. Blend in molasses and water.

Gradually stir dry ingredients into creamed mixture, blending well. Spread mixture in greased 13x9x2″ baking pan.

Bake in 350° oven 25 minutes or until cake tester or wooden pick inserted in center comes out clean. Cool completely in pan on rack.

Frost with Confectioners' Sugar Icing. To serve, cut into 2¼″ squares. Makes 24 squares.

CONFECTIONERS' SUGAR ICING:
Combine 1½ c. sifted confectioners' sugar, 5 tsp. milk and ½ tsp. vanilla in bowl. Beat until smooth, using a spoon.

Stuffed Cherry Tomatoes*

Leg of Lamb*

Butternut Squash and Peas*

Herbed French Bread*

Hot Apple Pie

Holidays and family celebrations call for especially good things to eat. Don't let your guests fill up on empty calories while they wait for the main course—offer them cherry tomatoes with a delicious filling of cream cheese and herbs. A leg of lamb looks impressive, but it's simple to prepare on the grill. The bright color combination of Butternut Squash and Peas will brighten any table. Herbed French Bread is flavored with lots of Parmesan cheese, garlic and just a sprinkling of oregano—a toasty taste sensation.

Stuffed Cherry Tomatoes

2 pt. cherry tomatoes (about 60)
Herb Filling (recipe follows)
paprika (optional)

IN ADVANCE:
Cut a thin slice from the top of each tomato and loosen the pulp, using a sharp knife. Remove pulp, using the handle of a teaspoon, and discard. Drain tomatoes, upside down, on paper towels. Set aside.

Prepare Herb Filling. Pipe mixture into tomato halves, using a pastry bag with a medium star tip (#32), or a measuring teaspoon. Sprinkle with paprika if you wish. Cover and refrigerate up to 6 hours before serving. Makes 60 appetizers.

HERB FILLING: Combine 2 (8-oz.) pkg. cream cheese (softened), ¼ c. minced fresh parsley, 2 tblsp. grated onion, 2 small cloves garlic (minced), and ¼ tsp. dried tarragon leaves in bowl. Beat until smooth, using an electric mixer.

Leg of Lamb

Peppery Chili Sauce (recipe follows)
¼ c. butter or regular margarine, melted
1 tblsp. lemon juice
¾ tsp. dried marjoram leaves
5 to 5½-lb. leg of lamb, boned and
* butterflied*

IN ADVANCE:
Prepare Peppery Chili Sauce.
TO GRILL:
Combine butter, lemon juice and marjoram in bowl; set aside.

Grill lamb 4" from gray coals (medium heat), turning often and basting with butter mixture. Cook 1 hour and 15 minutes or to desired doneness.

Meanwhile, warm sauce in a 2-qt. saucepan over medium heat until hot and bubbly. Remove from heat. Serve lamb with warm Peppery Chili Sauce. Makes 12 servings.

PEPPERY CHILI SAUCE: Heat ¼ c. butter or regular margarine in a 2-qt. saucepan over low heat until bubbly but not browned. Sauté ¾ c. chopped onion and ¾ c. chopped green pepper in butter until tender but not browned. Add 1¼ c. chili sauce, 3 tblsp. cider vinegar, 1 tblsp. Worcestershire sauce, 1 tblsp. brown sugar (packed), 1 tsp. Tabasco sauce, 1 tsp. dry mustard and ¼ tsp. pepper. Cook over high heat until mixture comes to a boil.

Reduce heat to low and simmer, uncovered, 30 minutes. Remove from heat and serve with lamb; or cover and refrigerate, then warm just before serving. Makes 2 c. sauce.

Butternut Squash and Peas

3 medium butternut squash (about
* 4½ lb. total)*
1 tsp. salt
2 (10-oz.) pkg. frozen peas (4 c.)
6 tblsp. butter or regular margarine

Pare the squash and remove seeds. Cut into 1" chunks. Set aside. Bring 1" of water and salt in Dutch oven to a boil over high heat. Add squash. Return water to a boil. Reduce heat to medium; cover and cook 10 minutes.

Add peas. Cook, covered, 5 to 7 minutes more or until vegetables are tender. Drain well. Add butter. Toss lightly to mix well. Makes 12 servings.

Herbed French Bread

½ c. butter or regular margarine,
* softened*
⅓ c. grated Parmesan cheese
2 cloves garlic, minced
½ tsp. dried oregano leaves
1 (20") loaf French bread

IN ADVANCE:
Combine butter, Parmesan cheese, garlic and oregano in bowl. Mix well. Set aside. Cut French bread into 1" slices. Spread slices with butter mixture. Reassemble slices to form a loaf on a 28" length of heavy-duty foil. Securely wrap loaf into a tight packet and refrigerate.
TO GRILL:
Heat bread 4" from gray coals (medium heat), turning occasionally, about 5 minutes or until butter mixture is melted and bread is hot. Makes 1 loaf.

Butter-Barbecued Beef Loaves*

Herbed Green Beans*

Lentil Salad*

Cinnamon Pears*

Saying goodbye to summer fun is hard for many children, so help ease the way for your youngsters with a fun-filled cookout. Butter-Barbecued Beef Loaves are wrapped and grilled in individual foil packets. Each mini-loaf contains ⅓ pound of meat—a generous serving for even the most high-spirited young students. Herbed Green Beans cook on the grill alongside the meat. Lentil Salad is a mélange of rice, lentils, tomato, green pepper, celery, olives and parsley, seasoned with bottled Italian dressing. For dessert, fresh Bartlett pears are sprinkled with brown sugar and cinnamon and cooked on the grill.

Butter-Barbecued Beef Loaves

Butter Barbecue Sauce (recipe follows)
2 lb. ground beef
½ c. cracker crumbs
⅓ c. chopped green pepper
¼ c. milk
¼ c. ketchup
1 tsp. salt
¼ tsp. pepper
2 eggs, slightly beaten
6 onion slices

IN ADVANCE:

Prepare Butter Barbecue Sauce.

Combine ground beef, cracker crumbs, green pepper, milk, ketchup, salt, pepper and eggs in bowl. Mix lightly, but well. Divide mixture into 6 equal portions and shape each portion into a loaf.

Place each loaf on a 12″ length of heavy-duty foil. Top each loaf with one onion slice and 3 tblsp. Butter Barbecue Sauce. Securely wrap each loaf into a loose packet and refrigerate.

TO GRILL:

Cook loaf packets 4″ from gray coals (medium heat). Cook 15 minutes, turn, and cook 15 minutes more or until done. Makes 6 servings.

BUTTER BARBECUE SAUCE: Heat ½ c. butter or regular margarine in 2-qt. saucepan until bubbly but not browned. Add ½ c. chopped onion and sauté until tender.

Add ½ c. ketchup, ¼ c. brown sugar (packed), 3 tblsp. Worcestershire sauce, 1½ tsp. chili powder, 1 tsp. salt, ⅛ tsp. pepper and a dash of Tabasco sauce. Mix well. Increase heat to high and cook until mixture comes to a boil.

Reduce heat to low and simmer 5 minutes. Remove from heat. Pour sauce into a bowl; cover and refrigerate.

Herbed Green Beans

4 c. cut green beans (1½″ lengths) or
  1 (20-oz.) bag frozen cut green beans
½ c. thinly sliced celery
½ c. chopped green pepper
¼ tsp. salt
4 tblsp. butter or regular margarine
1 large bay leaf

IN ADVANCE:
Combine green beans, celery, green pepper and salt on an 18″ length of heavy-duty foil. Mix lightly, but well. Top with butter and bay leaf. Securely wrap mixture into a loose packet and refrigerate.
TO GRILL:
Cook bean packet 4″ from gray coals (medium heat) 30 minutes, turning often. Makes 6 servings.

Lentil Salad

1½ c. water
½ c. dried lentils, rinsed and drained
1 tsp. salt
1 c. cooked rice
½ c. bottled Italian salad dressing
½ c. chopped tomato
¼ c. chopped green pepper
2 tblsp. chopped celery
2 tblsp. sliced pimiento-stuffed olives
chopped fresh parsley

IN ADVANCE:
Combine water, lentils and salt in 2-qt. saucepan. Cook over high heat until mixture comes to a boil. Reduce heat to low.
Cover and simmer 20 minutes or until lentils are tender. Remove from heat and drain.
Combine lentils, rice and salad dressing in bowl. Toss lightly to mix well.

Cover and refrigerate at least 3 hours before serving.
TO SERVE:
Stir tomato, green pepper, celery and olives into lentil-rice mixture. Sprinkle with parsley. Makes 3½ c. or 6 servings.

Cinnamon Pears

6 Bartlett pears, pared, cored and halved
6 tblsp. brown sugar, packed
3 tblsp. butter or regular margarine
6 tsp. water
ground cinnamon

IN ADVANCE:
Cut 6 (12″) lengths of foil and place two pear halves on each one. Top each with 1 tblsp. brown sugar, ½ tblsp. butter and sprinkle with 1 tsp. water. Securely wrap each portion into a loose packet and refrigerate.
TO GRILL:
Cook pears 4″ from light gray coals (low heat). Grill 20 minutes, without turning, or until pears are tender. To serve, sprinkle with cinnamon. Makes 6 servings.

Easy Salmon Chowder*

Barbecued Beef Buns*

Tomato Cups*

Old-fashioned Applesauce Cake*

Cranberry-Apple Cider*

Somehow the fall foliage seems even more beautiful viewed from the bow of a canoe or the deck of a sailboat—but even if you're landlocked, you can enjoy some of the atmosphere of a shore dinner. This shortcut chowder recipe takes advantage of convenience foods and yields a velvety-rich blend flecked with bacon bits. Hearty Barbecued Beef Buns, a recipe from a Washington wheat farmer's wife, can be made early in the day or even the day before. For a zesty salad that won't wilt, pack a big bowl of Tomato Cups. Old-fashioned Applesauce Cake is a light, moist cake chock-full of nuts and raisins; you can serve it right from the baking pan, so it's easy to tote. The aromatic hot Cranberry-Apple Cider is just the thing to ward off an early evening chill.

Easy Salmon Chowder

6 strips bacon, diced
½ c. chopped onion
1 (10¾-oz.) can condensed chicken broth
1 (5½-oz.) pkg. au gratin potato mix
2 c. water
1 (17-oz.) can whole-kernel corn
⅛ tsp. pepper
1 (15½-oz.) can red sockeye salmon, drained, boned, skinned and broken into chunks
1½ c. milk
⅓ c. evaporated milk

IN ADVANCE:

Fry bacon in 10″ skillet until crisp, about 8 minutes. Remove bacon and drain on paper towels.

Combine onion, chicken broth, au gratin potato mix (both potatoes and sauce mix), water, undrained corn and pepper with bacon in 3½-qt. slow cooker.

Cover and cook on low setting 6 hours. Add salmon, milk and evaporated milk.

Cover and cook on high setting 15 minutes or until thoroughly heated. Makes 9 c. or 8 servings.

Barbecued Beef Buns

4 c. cooked beef strips (2x¼″)
1 c. ketchup
½ c. cider vinegar
½ c. butter or regular margarine
¼ c. sugar
2 medium onions, thinly sliced
2 slices lemon
2 tblsp. Worcestershire sauce
4 tsp. prepared mustard
1 tsp. salt
¼ tsp. chili powder
¼ tsp. pepper
½ c. water
8 hamburger buns

Combine all ingredients except buns in 4-qt. Dutch oven. Cook over high heat until mixture comes to a boil. Reduce heat to low; simmer 25 minutes or until mixture thickens. Remove lemon slices. Pour into container, cover and refrigerate.

TO SERVE:
Warm over medium heat and serve in hamburger buns. Makes 8 servings.

Tomato Cups

5 medium tomatoes, chopped, or 3
  (28-oz.) cans tomatoes, drained
1½ c. green pepper strips (½")
1 medium onion, cut into rings
⅓ c. salad oil
2 tblsp. vinegar
1 tsp. salt
¾ tsp. dried oregano leaves
¾ tsp. dried basil leaves
¼ tsp. pepper

IN ADVANCE:
Combine all ingredients in bowl. Toss lightly to mix well. Cover and refrigerate. Makes 8 servings.

Old-fashioned Applesauce Cake

2½ c. sifted cake flour
1½ tsp. baking soda
¼ tsp. baking powder
1 tsp. salt
1 tsp. ground cinnamon
½ tsp. ground nutmeg
½ tsp. ground cloves
½ tsp. ground allspice
½ c. shortening
1¾ c. brown sugar, packed
2 eggs

1½ c. applesauce
½ c. water
1 c. raisins
1 c. chopped walnuts
confectioner's sugar

IN ADVANCE:
Sift together cake flour, baking soda, baking powder, salt, cinnamon, nutmeg, cloves and allspice; set aside.

Cream together shortening and brown sugar in mixing bowl until light and fluffy, using an electric mixer at medium speed. Add eggs one at a time, beating well after each addition.

Add dry ingredients alternately with applesauce and water to creamed mixture, beating well after each addition, using an electric mixer at low speed. Stir in raisins and walnuts. Pour batter into greased 13x9x2" baking pan.

Bake in 350° oven 45 minutes or until cake tester or wooden pick inserted in center comes out clean. Cool in pan on rack. Dust cake with confectioner's sugar. Makes 16 servings.

Cranberry-Apple Cider

1 qt. apple cider
1 qt. cranberry juice cocktail
½ tsp. ground allspice
½ tsp. ground cinnamon
½ tsp. ground cloves
¼ tsp. ground nutmeg

Combine all ingredients in 4-qt. Dutch oven. Warm over high heat until mixture comes to a boil. Remove from heat and serve. Makes 2 qt. or 8 (8-oz.) servings.

Main-Dish Potato Salad*

Zucchini Nut Bread*

Fresh Fruit

English Shortbread*

Lemon-Lime Freeze*

For most of us, the word picnic conjures up visions of an outdoor feast spread beneath a shade tree, but you can picnic just about anywhere: inside a cozy enclosed porch or greenhouse, in the family room—you're limited only by your imagination. Main-Dish Potato Salad is a meal in a bowl that brings open-air freshness indoors. While fresh zucchini is available, bake several loaves of Zucchini Nut Bread and freeze some for the busy days ahead. Our English Shortbread is an American adaptation, and it makes a sweet companion to Lemon-Lime Freeze.

Main-Dish Potato Salad

1 c. creamed small-curd cottage cheese
1 c. dairy sour cream
1 tblsp. prepared mustard
1 tblsp. sugar
1 tsp. salt
1/8 tsp. pepper
2 tblsp. chopped fresh parsley
2 lb. new potatoes, cooked,
  peeled and diced
2 c. fully cooked, cubed ham
1/2 c. sliced green onions
1/2 c. finely chopped celery
2 hard-cooked eggs, chopped
lettuce leaves
paprika

IN ADVANCE:
  Combine cottage cheese, sour cream, mustard, sugar, salt, pepper and parsley in bowl. Add potatoes, ham, green onions, celery and eggs. Toss to mix well. Cover and refrigerate several hours or until well chilled.
TO SERVE:
  Arrange salad on bed of lettuce and sprinkle with paprika. Makes 6 servings.

Zucchini Nut Bread

2 c. sifted flour
1 tsp. ground cinnamon
½ tsp. baking soda
½ tsp. salt
¼ tsp. baking powder
2 eggs
1⅓ c. sugar
⅔ c. cooking oil
2 tsp. vanilla
1⅓ c. shredded zucchini
½ c. chopped pecans
confectioners' sugar

IN ADVANCE:

Sift together flour, cinnamon, baking soda, salt and baking powder; set aside.

Beat eggs in bowl until blended, using an electric mixer at medium speed. Gradually add sugar and oil, mixing well after each addition. Blend in vanilla.

Add dry ingredients all at once, using an electric mixer at low speed. Stir in zucchini and pecans. Pour batter into greased 9x5x3″ loaf pan.

Bake in 350° oven 1 hour 15 minutes or until a cake tester inserted in center comes out clean. Cool in pan on rack 10 minutes. Remove from pan. Cool completely on rack.

Sprinkle with confectioners' sugar. Makes 1 loaf.

English Shortbread

3 c. sifted flour
1 tsp. baking powder
1 c. butter or regular margarine
½ c. sugar
1 egg

IN ADVANCE:

Sift together flour and baking powder; set aside.

Cream together butter and sugar in bowl until light and fluffy, using an electric mixer at medium speed. Beat in egg.

Add dry ingredients to creamed mixture, stirring well to blend. Knead dough lightly until it holds together.

Roll out dough on floured surface to 14″ square. Cut into 49 (2″) squares. Place squares about 2″ apart on ungreased baking sheets. Prick each with fork.

Bake in 325° oven 12 minutes or until lightly browned. Remove from baking sheets; cool on racks. Makes 4 doz. cookies.

Lemon-Lime Freeze

1 qt. lemonade
1 qt. lime sherbet

Combine half of the lemonade and half of the sherbet in a blender jar. Cover; blend at high speed until smooth. Pour into glasses. Repeat with remaining ingredients. Makes 6 (8-oz.) servings.

Marinated Pork Roast*

Kidney Bean Salad*

Apple-Walnut Mold*

Frosty Strawberry Torte*

N o matter how you slice it, pork tastes terrific cooked over the grill, and it cooks on a spit with almost no attention—just remember to baste it occasionally. A marinade of honey and soy sauce gives the meat a rich dark glaze. Salads always rate high at barbecues, and a Wisconsin farm wife tells us that relatives at her family picnics check to see if she's brought her special Kidney Bean Salad before they even say hello. The grand finale to this menu is an ultra-creamy dessert made with frozen strawberries and cream cheese that can be prepared indoors on a rainy day a month before the picnic.

Marinated Pork Roast

½ c. soy sauce
¼ c. honey
2 cloves garlic, minced
3 lb. boneless pork roast

IN ADVANCE:

Combine soy sauce, honey and garlic in glass bowl. Mix well. Add pork roast, turning to coat all sides. Cover and refrigerate 3 days, turning occasionally.

TO GRILL:

Insert spit through center of roast and secure tightly with holding forks. Place on gas grill rotisserie, close lid and grill over medium-low coals, basting often with marinade. Cook 2 hours, or until no longer pink in center, or until temperature on meat thermometer reaches 170°.

Let pork stand 15 minutes before serving. Makes 8 to 10 servings.

Kidney Bean Salad

5 (15-oz.) cans red kidney beans, drained
1 c. chopped onion
½ c. chopped celery
⅓ c. sweet pickle relish
½ c. cider vinegar
½ c. sugar
1 egg, slightly beaten
2 tsp. dry mustard

IN ADVANCE:

Combine kidney beans, onion, celery and pickle relish in bowl. Set aside.

Combine vinegar, sugar, egg and mustard in 1-qt. saucepan; mix well. Cook over low heat, stirring constantly, 7 minutes or until mixture thickens. Remove from heat.

Pour vinegar mixture over vegetables,

tossing gently to coat well. Cover and refrigerate at least 6 hours before serving. Makes 8 to 10 servings.

Apple-Walnut Mold

2 env. unflavored gelatin
4 c. apple juice
2 tblsp. lemon juice
2 c. chopped red apples
½ c. shredded, pared carrots
½ c. thinly sliced celery
½ c. chopped walnuts
¼ c. raisins
Honey Dressing (recipe follows)

IN ADVANCE:

Soften gelatin in ½ c. apple juice in 2-qt. saucepan. Add remaining apple juice and cook over low heat until gelatin is completely dissolved. Stir in lemon juice. Refrigerate 45 to 60 minutes or until thick and syrupy.

Fold in apple, carrot, celery, walnuts and raisins. Pour into 6-c. mold.

Refrigerate 2 to 2½ hours or until set. Meanwhile, prepare Honey Dressing. Refrigerate.

TO SERVE:

Unmold gelatin and spoon Honey Dressing over top. Makes 8 to 10 servings.

HONEY DRESSING: Combine ½ c. mayonnaise, 1 tblsp. honey and 1 tblsp. lemon juice in bowl. Mix well.

Frosty Strawberry Torte

2 (10-oz.) pkg. frozen strawberries, thawed
1 env. unflavored gelatin
1 (8-oz.) pkg. cream cheese, softened
1 (7½-oz.) jar marshmallow creme
1 tblsp. hot water
20 ladyfingers, split
2 (1½-oz.) env. whipped topping mix
2 (11-oz.) cans mandarin orange segments, drained
1 (8½-oz.) can pear halves, diced and drained
1 (3½-oz.) can flaked coconut

IN ADVANCE:

Drain juice from strawberries into a 2-qt. saucepan, reserving strawberries. Sprinkle gelatin over juice. Cook over low heat, stirring constantly, until gelatin is completely dissolved. Chill until syrupy, about 30 minutes.

Combine cream cheese, marshmallow creme and hot water in bowl. Beat 1 minute, using an electric mixer at low speed. Beat at high speed 2 minutes more or until thick and creamy. Fold in gelatin mixture.

Chill until mixture mounds slightly when dropped from a spoon, about 30 minutes.

Line bottom and sides of 9″ springform pan with ladyfingers. Using a large bowl, prepare whipped topping mix according to package directions. Fold in gelatin mixture. Then gently fold in oranges, pears, coconut and strawberries.

Pour into prepared pan. Cover with plastic wrap. Wrap in foil. Freeze until firm. May be stored in freezer up to 4 weeks.

TO SERVE:

Unwrap and let stand 30 minutes at room temperature before slicing. Makes 12 servings.

Parslied Chicken Chowder*

Special Chef's Salad*

Pumpernickel Loaves

Apricot Bars*

Build a tailgate picnic around an easy-to-assemble menu of soup and salad. Hot Parslied Chicken Chowder—a savory soup rich in potatoes, carrots and chicken—cooks in a snap on top of the range. Special Chef's Salad, a crisp mixture of garden vegetables topped with a simple vinaigrette, is the perfect partner. Wedges of pumpernickel help balance the meal by adding extra color, texture and nutrition. The apricot bar cookies have a citrus-flavored icing made with both lemon and orange.

Parslied Chicken Chowder

2 tblsp. butter or regular margarine
¼ c. chopped onion
1½ c. cubed, cooked chicken (1″)
1½ c. cubed, pared potatoes (½″)
1½ c. cubed, pared carrots (¼″)
2 chicken bouillon cubes
1 tsp. salt
⅛ tsp. pepper
2 c. water
3 tblsp. flour
2½ c. milk
chopped fresh parsley

IN ADVANCE:
Melt butter over low heat in a 3-qt. saucepan. Cook onion in butter until tender.

Add chicken, potatoes, carrots, bouillon cubes, salt, pepper and water. Cover and cook over high heat until mixture comes to a boil. Reduce heat to low and simmer 20 minutes or until vegetables are tender.

Meanwhile, combine flour and ½ c. of the milk in jar. Cover and shake until blended and smooth. Stir flour mixture and remaining 2 c. milk into vegetable-chicken mixture. Cook over medium heat, stirring constantly, until mixture boils and thickens.

Remove from heat and pour into thermos jar.
TO SERVE:
Sprinkle with parsley. Makes 1¾ qt. or 6 servings.

Special Chef's Salad

2 c. bite-size pieces lettuce
2 c. bite-size pieces spinach
½ c. chopped green pepper
½ c. shredded, pared carrots
½ c. halved cucumber slices
½ lb. fully cooked ham, cut into strips
  (1 c.)
1 (3-oz.) pkg. cream cheese, cubed
2 hard-cooked eggs, chopped
1 small onion, sliced
Oil and Vinegar Dressing (recipe follows)

IN ADVANCE:

Combine lettuce, spinach, green pepper, carrots, cucumber, ham, cream cheese, eggs and onion in a large bowl. Cover and refrigerate.

Prepare Oil and Vinegar Dressing; cover and refrigerate.

TO SERVE:

Pour Oil and Vinegar Dressing over salad ingredients. Toss gently. Makes 6 servings.

OIL AND VINEGAR DRESSING: Combine ½ c. salad oil, ¼ c. vinegar, 1 tblsp. ketchup, ¾ tsp. sugar, ¾ tsp. salt, ½ tsp. garlic salt and ⅛ tsp. pepper in jar. Cover tightly and shake well. Makes ¾ c.

Apricot Bars

1 c. boiling water
1 c. dried apricots
1¾ c. sifted flour
1 tsp. baking powder
¾ tsp. salt
½ c. butter or regular margarine
2 c. brown sugar, packed
2 eggs
1 tsp. vanilla
1 tsp. grated orange rind
Orange Icing (recipe follows)
½ c. chopped walnuts

IN ADVANCE:

Pour boiling water over apricots in bowl. Let stand 5 minutes. Drain apricots and snip into small pieces. Set aside.

Sift together flour, baking powder and salt; set aside.

Cream together butter and brown sugar in bowl until light and fluffy, using an electric mixer at medium speed. Add eggs one at a time, beating well after each addition. Beat in vanilla and orange rind.

Gradually stir dry ingredients into creamed mixture, mixing well. Stir in apricots. Spread batter in greased 15½x10½x1″ jellyroll pan.

Bake in 350° oven 20 minutes, or until top springs back when touched lightly with finger. Cool in pan on rack 10 minutes. Meanwhile, prepare Orange Icing.

Spread warm bars with Orange Icing. Sprinkle with walnuts, pressing them in lightly so they adhere to icing. Cool completely. Cut into 2½x1½″ bars. Makes 48.

ORANGE ICING: Combine 1 c. sifted confectioners' sugar, 2 tsp. soft butter or regular margarine, 1 tsp. grated orange rind, 2 tsp. orange juice and 2 tsp. lemon juice in bowl. Stir until smooth.

OCTOBERFEST

Bratwurst and Onions*

Frankfurter Buns*

German Potato Salad*

Apples Alfresco*

Chilled Apple Cider

Y*ou can almost hear the oom-pah-pah of a Bavarian band when you celebrate Octoberfest with such traditional food as bratwurst-and-onion sandwiches on homemade buns. As you'd expect, we've included a warm German Potato Salad, too. Apples Alfresco, cooked and served in their own little foil bowls, make a wonderful finale. These individual desserts combine tart apples with spicy cinnamon candies and taste simply delicious. They're even better served with heavy cream or vanilla ice cream.*

Bratwurst and Onions

4 c. sliced onion
3 tblsp. cooking oil
2 tblsp. water
4½ tsp. paprika
¼ tsp. ground cumin (optional)
6 strips bacon
6 bratwurst (2 lb.)
Frankfurter Buns (recipe follows)

IN ADVANCE:
Combine onion, oil, water, paprika and cumin; mix well. Place on a 20″ length of heavy-duty foil. Securely wrap mixture into a loose packet and refrigerate.

Wrap one bacon strip around each bratwurst, securing bacon with wooden picks. Cover and refrigerate.

TO GRILL:
Cook onion packet and bratwurst 4″ from gray coals (medium heat), turning bratwurst often. Grill 20 to 25 minutes or until onions are tender and bratwurst is cooked through.

To serve, place bratwurst in Frankfurter Buns and top with onions. Makes 6 sandwiches.

Frankfurter Buns

2 c. milk
¾ c. sugar
⅔ c. lard
3 tsp. salt
2 pkg. active dry yeast
1 tsp. sugar
1 c. lukewarm water (110°)
10½ to 11 c. sifted flour
2 eggs

IN ADVANCE:
Scald milk in 1-qt. saucepan over medium heat. Meanwhile, combine ¾ c.

sugar, lard and salt in large mixing bowl; set aside. Pour milk over sugar mixture. Cool to lukewarm.

Sprinkle yeast and 1 tsp. sugar over lukewarm water, stirring to dissolve. Let stand 10 minutes.

Add yeast mixture, 5 c. of the flour and eggs to milk mixture. Beat about 2 minutes, using an electric mixer at medium speed. Gradually stir in enough remaining flour to make a soft dough.

Turn dough out onto floured surface. Knead until smooth and satiny, 8 to 10 minutes. Place dough in greased bowl.

Cover and let rise in warm place until doubled, about 1 hour.

Punch down dough and divide into fourths. Let rest 10 minutes.

Roll each fourth into a 9x4″ rectangle. Cut in 9 (4x1″) strips. Roll each strip to form a 5½″ cylinder.

Place on greased baking sheets, about 3″ apart. Flatten slightly with the palm of your hand. Cover and let rise until doubled, about 45 minutes.

Bake in 350° oven 18 minutes or until golden brown. Remove from baking sheets and cool on racks. When cooled completely, wrap in foil until ready to use. Makes 36 buns.

German Potato Salad

5 medium all-purpose potatoes
5 strips bacon
½ c. chopped onion
2 tblsp. sugar
1 tblsp. flour
1½ tsp. salt
¼ tsp. pepper
½ c. water
¼ c. vinegar
½ c. sliced radishes

Cook unpared potatoes in boiling water in Dutch oven 25 to 35 minutes or until tender. Drain in colander and cool slightly.

Meanwhile, fry bacon over medium heat 5 minutes or until crisp. Remove bacon and drain on paper towels. Crumble bacon and set aside. Sauté onion in pan drippings 5 minutes or until partially tender.

Combine sugar, flour, salt, pepper, ½ c. water and vinegar. Mix until well blended and smooth. Add to onion mixture. Cook, stirring constantly, until mixture boils and thickens, about 2 minutes. Remove from heat. Carefully peel and slice warm potatoes; add to onion mixture. Cook potato-onion mixture over medium heat, about 2 minutes or until hot and bubbly.

Remove potato-onion mixture from heat. Add radishes and toss lightly to mix well. Sprinkle with bacon. Makes 6 servings.

Apples Alfresco

6 tart apples
1 (8-oz.) can pineapple chunks, drained
6 tblsp. brown sugar, packed
¼ c. lemon juice
2 tblsp. red cinnamon candies

IN ADVANCE:
Core apples and score the top half of each one, using the tines of a fork. Place each apple on an 8″ length of heavy-duty foil. Fill the cavity of each apple with 2 chunks of pineapple, 1 tblsp. brown sugar, 2 tsp. lemon juice and 1 tsp. candies.

Securely wrap each apple into a loose packet and refrigerate.
TO GRILL:
Cook apple packets 4″ from gray coals (medium heat), turning once or twice. Grill 30 to 40 minutes or until tender. Makes 6 servings.

Texican Chili*

Mexican Salad Bowl*

Cheesy Bacon-Corn Muffins*

Family-style Cookies*

Most ranchers' wives have a fat file of recipes for straightforward, hearty food—and plenty of it!—designed to please man-sized appetites. These four dishes are simple to prepare and will provide a casual, satisfying meal served just about anywhere. Fill a slow cooker with Texican Chili, a spicy beef-and-bean mixture with chunky cubes of beef. When you bite into Cheesy Bacon-Corn Muffins, you'll discover crisp bacon bits and golden nuggets of melted Cheddar. Mexican Salad Bowl is sprinkled with cheese and corn chips, then tossed with a creamy dressing made with fresh avocados. The big-batch recipe for Family-style Cookies has something for every taste—apples and oranges, raisins and nuts, and even a cup of carrots.

Texican Chili

6 strips bacon, diced
2 lb. boneless beef round, cut into
 ½" cubes
2 (15-oz.) cans kidney beans, drained
1 (28-oz.) can tomatoes, cut up
1 (8-oz.) can tomato sauce
1 c. finely chopped onion
½ c. thinly sliced, pared carrots
½ c. finely chopped green pepper
½ c. finely chopped celery
2 tblsp. minced fresh parsley
2 cloves garlic, minced
1 bay leaf
2 tblsp. chili powder
1 tsp. salt
½ tsp. ground cumin
⅛ tsp. pepper

IN ADVANCE:

Fry bacon in 10" skillet over medium heat 5 minutes or until crisp. Remove and drain on paper towels.

Brown half the beef cubes in pan drippings 5 minutes. Place in 3½-qt. slow cooker. Repeat with remaining beef cubes. Stir bacon and remaining ingredients into slow cooker.

Cover and cook on low setting 10 to 12 hours or until beef is tender. Makes 6 servings.

Mexican Salad Bowl

8 c. bite-size mixed greens
¼ c. chopped green onion
¼ c. chopped green pepper
¼ c. sliced, pitted ripe olives
2 tomatoes, cut into wedges
Avocado Salad Dressing (recipe follows)
¼ c. shredded Cheddar cheese
1 c. coarsely crushed corn chips

IN ADVANCE:

Combine greens, green onion, green pepper, olives and tomatoes in salad bowl. Cover and refrigerate. Prepare Avocado Salad Dressing.

TO SERVE:

Sprinkle salad ingredients with cheese, then corn chips. Top with Avocado Salad Dressing and toss lightly. Makes 6 to 8 servings.

AVOCADO SALAD DRESSING: Mash 1 avocado with 2 tblsp. lemon juice. Combine with ½ c. dairy sour cream, ¼ c. salad oil, 1 tsp. seasoned salt and ¼ tsp. chili powder. Cover and refrigerate several hours before serving.

Cheesy Bacon-Corn Muffins

8 strips bacon, diced
¼ c. chopped onion
1¼ c. sifted flour
¾ c. yellow corn meal
½ c. sugar
3 tsp. baking powder
1 tsp. salt
2 eggs, beaten
1 c. milk
3 tblsp. butter or regular margarine, melted
½ c. shredded Cheddar cheese

IN ADVANCE:

Fry bacon and onion in 10″ skillet over medium heat 5 minutes or until bacon is browned. Remove bacon and onion and drain on paper towels.

Sift together flour, corn meal, sugar, baking powder and salt into bowl.

Combine eggs, milk and butter in another bowl; mix well. Add egg mixture all at once to dry ingredients, stirring just until moistened. Stir in bacon-onion mixture and cheese. Spoon batter into greased 3″ muffin-pan cups, filling two-thirds full.

Bake in 400° oven 15 minutes or until wooden pick inserted in center of muffin comes out clean. Cool completely

and wrap in foil (or serve immediately). Makes 12 muffins.

TO REHEAT:

Heat foil-wrapped muffins in 350° oven 10 to 12 minutes.

Family-style Cookies

1 c. cut-up, pared carrots
1 large apple, cored and cut into wedges
1 large orange, cut into wedges (not peeled)
1 c. cut-up pitted dates
1 c. raisins
4½ c. sifted flour
1 tsp. baking soda
1 tsp. ground cinnamon
½ tsp. salt
½ tsp. ground nutmeg
¼ tsp. ground allspice
¼ tsp. ground cloves
1 c. butter or regular margarine
2 c. sugar
3 eggs
1 c. chopped walnuts

IN ADVANCE:

Grind carrots, apple, orange, dates and raisins in food grinder, using medium blade. Set aside.

Sift together flour, baking soda, cinnamon, salt, nutmeg, allspice and cloves; set aside.

Cream together butter and sugar in bowl until light and fluffy, using an electric mixer at medium speed. Add eggs one at a time, beating well after each addition.

Gradually stir dry ingredients into creamed mixture, mixing well. Stir in ground fruit mixture and walnuts. Drop mixture by teaspoonfuls, about 2″ apart, on greased baking sheets.

Bake in 350° oven 10 to 12 minutes or until golden brown. Remove from baking sheets; cool on racks. Makes 7½ doz. cookies.

Herbed Split Turkey*

Grill-baked Sweet Potatoes*

Buttered Broccoli Spears

Cranberry-Orange Salad*

Pumpkin Cheese Pie*

I f the weather is kind, there's no reason your holiday turkey can't be cooked outdoors. Herbed Split Turkey is grilled over slow coals and basted with a mixture of oil, lemon juice, parsley and sage, so it stays moist and flavorful. Grill-baked Sweet Potatoes are foil-wrapped and grilled over the coals. Cranberry-Orange Salad, a tangy combination with chopped walnuts to add crunch, is soft-set in a gelatin base and refrigerated until serving time. For a new-fashioned dessert, bake a Pumpkin Cheese Pie; it has the creamy texture of cheesecake with the all-American taste of pumpkin pie.

Herbed Split Turkey

¼ c. cooking oil
2 tblsp. minced fresh parsley
2 tsp. dried rubbed sage
2 tsp. lemon juice
1 (8 to 10-lb.) turkey, split

TO GRILL:
Combine cooking oil, parsley, sage and lemon juice in bowl; mix well.
Grill turkey halves, skin side down, 4" from gray coals (medium heat), turning often with tongs and basting with herb mixture. Cook 1 hour 30 minutes or until meat thermometer inserted in the thickest part of thigh registers 185°. Makes 6 servings plus leftovers.

Grill-baked Sweet Potatoes

6 sweet potatoes
butter or regular margarine

IN ADVANCE:
Pierce tops of sweet potatoes with a fork and place each potato on a 12" length of heavy-duty foil. Securely wrap each potato into a loose packet.
TO GRILL:
Cook potatoes 4" from light gray coals (low heat), turning often with tongs. Grill 25 to 35 minutes or until tender. Split open and top each with a pat of butter. Makes 6 servings.

Cranberry-Orange Salad

2 c. cranberries, fresh or frozen
1 orange, quartered and seeded
¾ c. sugar
1 env. unflavored gelatin
1 c. cranberry juice cocktail
¼ c. chopped walnuts

IN ADVANCE:

Grind cranberries and orange into a bowl, using medium blade of food grinder. Add sugar; mix well. Set aside.

Sprinkle gelatin over ½ c. of the cranberry juice in a 1-qt. saucepan. Let stand 5 minutes to soften. Heat over low heat until gelatin is completely dissolved.

Stir dissolved gelatin, remaining cranberry juice and walnuts into cranberry-orange mixture. Turn into serving bowl.

Chill several hours or until set. Makes 6 servings.

Pumpkin Cheese Pie

1½ c. graham cracker crumbs
½ tsp. pumpkin pie spice
⅓ c. butter or regular margarine, melted
12 oz. cream cheese, softened
¾ c. brown sugar, packed
2 tblsp. flour
1 tsp. pumpkin pie spice
1 tsp. grated lemon rind
¼ tsp. vanilla
3 eggs
1 c. cooked or canned mashed pumpkin
¾ c. dairy sour cream
1 tblsp. sugar
¼ tsp. vanilla

IN ADVANCE:

Combine graham cracker crumbs and ½ tsp. pumpkin pie spice in bowl. Add butter to crumb mixture. Mix well. Press crumb mixture into bottom and up sides of 9″ pie plate. Set aside.

Cream together cream cheese and brown sugar in bowl, using an electric mixer at medium speed. Add flour, 1 tsp. pumpkin pie spice, lemon juice and ¼ tsp. vanilla; beat until smooth. Add eggs one at a time, beating well after each addition. Stir in pumpkin; mix until well blended. Pour into prepared crust.

Bake in 325° oven 40 minutes or until set in center.

Meanwhile, combine sour cream, sugar and ¼ tsp. vanilla. Spread over baked cheesecake. Cool on rack 1 hour.

Cover and refrigerate at least 3 hours before serving. Makes 10 servings.

VARIATION: To microwave, prepare crust and filling as for oven method. Microwave (medium setting) 18 minutes, rotating pie one-quarter turn every three minutes. Prepare topping and continue as for oven method.

Ham Barbecue Sandwiches*

Super Baked Beans*

Kathy's Hot Water Chocolate Cake*

Frothy Mocha Cocoa*

American Indians on the Northwest coast started the tradition of the potlatch, and it was a social occasion for celebration and gift-giving. But a potlatch needn't be elaborate—sometimes just finding time to share a meal with friends is reason enough for celebration. A Washington farm woman says that these Ham Barbecue Sandwiches are among her family's favorites, and she likes them because they're so convenient. The filling can be prepared and refrigerated, then heated and served right in the buns. Super Baked Beans are simmered on top of the range, then baked several hours in a flavorful sauce of tomatoes, molasses and lemon-lime soda. Serve the chocolate cake with mugs of Frothy Mocha Cocoa—a rich blend of chocolate, coffee and cream—for a double chocolate treat.

Ham Barbecue Sandwiches

1½ lb. cooked ham, chopped
1½ c. ketchup
2 tblsp. cider vinegar
2 tblsp. brown sugar, packed
1 tblsp. prepared mustard
1 tblsp. Worcestershire sauce
8 frankfurter rolls

IN ADVANCE:
Combine all ingredients except frankfurter rolls in 2-qt. saucepan. Cook over medium heat until mixture comes to a boil. Remove from heat. Cover and refrigerate.
TO GRILL:
Place each frankfurter roll on a 10" length of heavy-duty foil. Fill each roll with about ⅓ c. ham mixture. Securely wrap each roll into a loose packet.
Grill packets 4" from gray coals (medium heat). Cook 20 minutes, turning often with tongs. Makes 8 servings.

Super Baked Beans

1 lb. dried navy beans
water
1 (28-oz.) can tomatoes, cut up
1 (12-oz.) can lemon-lime-flavored soda
¼ c. water
6 strips bacon, cut into 1" pieces
1 tsp. salt
½ tsp. pepper
1 (8-oz.) can tomato sauce
¾ c. chopped onion
¾ c. chopped celery
½ c. chopped green pepper
½ c. molasses
½ c. ketchup
⅓ c. brown sugar, packed
1 tblsp. prepared mustard

1 tblsp. Worcestershire sauce
2 tsp. cider vinegar

IN ADVANCE:
Place beans in bowl. Add enough water to cover and soak overnight.

The next day, drain beans. Combine beans, tomatoes, lemon-lime soda, ¼ c. water, bacon, salt and pepper in 4-qt. Dutch oven. Cook over high heat until mixture comes to a boil. Reduce heat to low. Cover and simmer 1 hour.

Stir in remaining ingredients. Cover and simmer 1 hour more.

Pour hot bean mixture into 3-qt. casserole. Cover and bake in 250° oven 4 hours.

Uncover and bake 30 minutes more, or until beans are tender. Makes 8 servings.

Kathy's Hot Water Chocolate Cake

2 c. sifted flour
½ c. baking cocoa
2 tsp. baking soda
½ tsp. salt
½ c. butter or regular margarine
1½ c. sugar
2 eggs
½ c. milk
1 tsp. vanilla
1 c. boiling water
Fluffy Chocolate Frosting (recipe follows)

IN ADVANCE:
Sift together flour, cocoa, baking soda and salt; set aside.

Cream together butter and sugar in bowl until light and fluffy, using an electric mixer at medium speed. Add eggs one at a time, beating well after each addition. Blend in milk and vanilla.

Stir in dry ingredients, using an electric mixer at low speed. Gradually add boiling water, stirring until smooth. Pour batter into greased 13x9x2" baking pan.

Bake in 325° oven 35 minutes or until cake tester inserted in center comes out clean. Cool in pan or rack. Frost cake with Fluffy Chocolate Frosting. Makes 16 servings.

FLUFFY CHOCOLATE FROSTING:
Melt 2 (1-oz.) squares unsweetened chocolate in saucepan over low heat. Cool. Combine 3 c. sifted confectioners' sugar, ⅓ c. butter or regular margarine (softened), 3 tblsp. milk, 1 tsp vanilla and melted chocolate in bowl. Beat until smooth.

Frothy Mocha Cocoa

4 (1-oz.) squares unsweetened chocolate
1 c. sugar
¼ c. instant coffee powder
1 c. water
3 c. milk
2 c. light cream
2 tsp. vanilla

IN ADVANCE:
Combine chocolate, sugar, coffee powder and water in 3-qt. saucepan. Cook over low heat, stirring constantly, until chocolate is melted.

Increase heat to medium. Cook until mixture boils. Reduce heat to low. Simmer 4 minutes, stirring occasionally.

Stir in milk, cream and vanilla. Heat 5 minutes or until hot. Remove from heat and beat with rotary beater until foamy.

Pour into thermos jugs. Makes 6 c. or 8 (6-oz.) servings.

Beef 'n' Egg Loaves*

Bacon-Cheese Macaroni*

Six-Vegetable Salad*

Peanut Butter Brownies*

Fresh Fruit

*A*t harvest time, it's almost impossible to get farmers to stop working long enough to come in for dinner, and many farm wives solve this seasonal problem by taking dinner to the field. The individual-sized Beef 'n' Egg Loaves are ground beef enriched with wheat germ. Each loaf is wrapped around a hard-cooked egg and spread with a mildly seasoned sauce. The quick Bacon-Cheese Macaroni starts with soup (no need to make a white sauce) and bakes alongside the meat loaves. To complement the main course, serve a cool, crunchy Six-Vegetable Salad. For dessert, pack a basket of rich Peanut Butter Brownies and an assortment of fresh fruit.

Beef 'n' Egg Loaves

1½ lb. ground beef
¼ c. wheat germ
¼ c. finely chopped onion
¼ c. chopped fresh parsley
1 tsp. salt
¼ tsp. dried thyme leaves
¼ tsp. dry mustard
¼ tsp. paprika
1 egg
¼ c. milk
¼ c. ketchup
6 hard-cooked eggs, peeled
Sweet-Sour Sauce (recipe follows)

IN ADVANCE:
Combine all ingredients except hard-cooked eggs and Sweet-Sour Sauce in bowl. Mix lightly, but well.

Divide mixture into 6 equal portions and gently press each portion around a hard-cooked egg, forming a loaf.

Place loaves in shallow roasting pan. Bake in 375° oven 20 minutes. Meanwhile, prepare Sweet-Sour Sauce and spoon over loaves. Bake 15 minutes more. Makes 6 servings.

SWEET-SOUR SAUCE: Combine ¼ c. ketchup, 1 tblsp. vinegar, 1 tblsp. brown sugar (packed) and ½ tsp. dry mustard in bowl; mix well.

Bacon-Cheese Macaroni

7 to 8 oz. elbow or corkscrew macaroni
6 strips bacon, cut into ½" pieces
½ c. chopped onion
1 (10¾-oz.) can condensed cream of mushroom soup
1 (4-oz.) can sliced mushrooms
⅔ c. milk
1½ c. shredded Longhorn-style mild Cheddar or Colby cheese
1½ c. shredded sharp Cheddar cheese

2 c. frozen peas, thawed
2 tblsp. diced pimiento
1 tblsp. chopped fresh parsley

Cook macaroni according to package directions for casseroles, but do not add salt. Meanwhile, cook bacon and onion over medium heat in 10″ skillet until bacon is crisp. Stir in soup, undrained mushrooms and milk. Remove from heat.

Drain hot macaroni in colander and return to kettle. Add soup mixture, cheese, peas, pimiento and parsley. Toss gently to mix. Turn into greased 2-qt. casserole.

Bake in 375° oven 35 minutes or until hot. Makes 6 servings.

Six-Vegetable Salad

⅓ c. salad oil
2 tblsp. cider vinegar
1 clove garlic, minced
¼ tsp. salt
¼ tsp. Worcestershire sauce
¼ tsp. paprika
1 medium unpared zucchini, cut in half
   lengthwise and sliced (1½ c.)
3 medium tomatoes, cut into 1″ chunks
1 green pepper, cut into 1″ strips
¾ c. shredded, pared carrots
½ c. sliced radishes
¼ c. sliced green onions
¼ c. chopped fresh parsley

IN ADVANCE:
Combine salad oil, vinegar, garlic, salt, Worcestershire sauce and paprika in jar. Cover and shake until well blended. Refrigerate.

TO SERVE:
Combine zucchini, tomatoes, green pepper, carrots, radishes, green onions and parsley in bowl. Pour dressing over vegetable mixture. Toss lightly to mix well. Makes 6 servings.

Peanut Butter Brownies

1⅓ c. sifted flour
⅛ tsp. baking soda
½ c. butter or regular margarine
1 c. sugar
2 eggs
1 tsp. vanilla
¾ c. chocolate-flavored syrup
1 c. peanut butter-flavored chips (6 oz.)
Peanut Butter Glaze (recipe follows)
¼ c. chopped peanuts
½ (1-oz.) square unsweetened chocolate,
   melted and cooled

IN ADVANCE:
Sift together flour and baking soda; set aside. Cream together butter and sugar in mixing bowl until light and fluffy, using an electric mixer at medium speed. Add eggs and vanilla, beating well.

Add dry ingredients alternately with syrup to creamed mixture, blending well after each addition, using an electric mixer at low speed. Stir in peanut butter chips. Spread mixture into greased 13x9x2″ baking pan.

Bake in 350° oven 30 to 35 minutes or until top springs back when touched lightly with finger. Cool completely in pan on rack.

Prepare Peanut Butter Glaze. Immediately pour over brownies, spreading quickly with a knife. Sprinkle with peanuts. Drizzle chocolate on top.

Cut into 2¼″ squares. Makes 24 brownies.

PEANUT BUTTER GLAZE: Combine ⅓ c. sugar, ¼ c. evaporated milk and 2 tblsp. butter or regular margarine in a 1-qt. saucepan. Cook over medium heat, stirring constantly, until mixture comes to a boil. Remove from heat. Add 1 c. peanut butter-flavored chips (6 oz.), stirring until melted. Blend in 1 tsp. vanilla.

Lemon-Rosemary Drumsticks*

Peas and Mushrooms*

Sweet Potato Salad*

Raspberry-Vanilla Cloud*

Becoming a gourmet at the grill needn't mean hours of fancy food preparation; the recipes in this menu are both elegant and easy. A simple side dish of peas and fresh mushrooms will be a nice accompaniment to Lemon-Rosemary Drumsticks. Marinated overnight and quickly cooked to a golden brown, the chicken drumsticks look especially inviting flecked with bits of rosemary. For an exotic salad, combine sweet potatoes, apples, celery and fresh orange segments with crunchy peanuts and a fruit-flavored dressing. Don't be reluctant to try Raspberry-Vanilla Cloud, a sensational refrigerator dessert in a graham cracker crust crowned with a ruby-red sauce.

Lemon-Rosemary Drumsticks

½ c. lemon juice
½ c. cooking oil
½ c. chopped onion
½ tsp. dried rosemary leaves
½ tsp. salt
⅛ tsp. pepper
18 chicken drumsticks

IN ADVANCE:
Combine all ingredients except chicken in bowl. Mix well. Arrange chicken in 12x8x2″ (2-qt.) glass baking dish. Pour marinade over chicken. Cover and refrigerate overnight.
TO GRILL:
Cook chicken 4″ from gray coals (medium heat), turning and basting often with marinade. Grill 30 minutes or until tender. Makes 6 servings.

Peas and Mushrooms

4 lb. fresh peas or 2 (10-oz.) pkg. frozen
   peas, thawed
½ c. thinly sliced fresh mushrooms
salt
pepper
4 tblsp. butter or regular margarine

IN ADVANCE:
If using fresh peas, shell peas by pressing pod between thumbs to open; remove peas, discard pods, and rinse thoroughly. Place peas on a 24″ length of foil. Top with mushrooms. Sprinkle with salt and pepper and dot with butter. Wrap securely into a packet.
TO GRILL:
Cook packet 4″ from gray coals (medium heat). Shifting packet occasionally, grill 20 minutes or until tender. Makes 6 servings.

Sweet Potato Salad

¼ c. sugar
1 tblsp. cornstarch
⅛ tsp. salt
1 c. pineapple juice
⅓ c. orange juice
3 tblsp. lemon juice
2 eggs, beaten
1 c. heavy cream, whipped
1½ c. unpared, diced apples
1½ c. thinly sliced celery
1½ c. cooked, diced sweet potatoes
1 c. orange sections
½ c. salted peanuts
lettuce leaves

IN ADVANCE:
Combine sugar, cornstarch and salt in 2-qt. saucepan. Stir in pineapple juice, orange juice and lemon juice. Cook over medium heat, stirring constantly, until mixture boils and thickens, about 2 minutes. Remove from heat.

Quickly stir a little of the hot mixture into the eggs. Stir egg mixture back into juice mixture and cook over low heat, stirring constantly, 2 minutes more.

Pour into bowl and cover with plastic wrap. Chill in refrigerator several hours or until cold.

TO SERVE:
Fold whipped cream into chilled juice mixture. Fold in apples, celery, sweet potatoes, orange sections and peanuts. Serve on lettuce leaves. Makes 5½ c. or 6 servings.

Raspberry-Vanilla Cloud

1⅔ c. graham cracker crumbs
¼ c. sugar
1 tsp. ground cinnamon
⅓ c. butter or regular margarine, melted
½ c. sugar
¼ c. flour
1 pkg. unflavored gelatin
½ tsp. salt
1¾ c. milk
3 egg whites
¼ tsp. cream of tartar
½ c. sugar
1 tsp. vanilla
½ c. heavy cream, whipped
Raspberry Sauce (recipe follows)

IN ADVANCE:
Mix together graham cracker crumbs, ¼ c. sugar, cinnamon and butter. Press into 9″ square baking pan. Bake in 375° oven 4 minutes. Cool on rack.

Combine ½ c. sugar, flour, gelatin and salt in 2-qt. saucepan. Slowly stir in milk. Cook over medium heat, stirring constantly, until mixture comes to a boil. Boil for 1 minute. Remove from heat and cool thoroughly.

Beat egg whites with cream of tartar in bowl until foamy, using an electric mixer at high speed. Gradually beat in ½ c. sugar. Add vanilla. Fold egg whites and whipped cream into cooled gelatin mixture. Turn into crust. Cover and refrigerate several hours or overnight.

Prepare Raspberry Sauce. Cover and refrigerate.

TO SERVE:
Cut into squares and serve topped with Raspberry Sauce. Makes 9 servings.

RASPBERRY SAUCE: Drain 2 (10-oz.) pkg. frozen raspberries (thawed). Add water to juice to make 1½ c. Combine juice, ¼ c. sugar, 2 tblsp. cornstarch and 1 tblsp. lemon juice in 2-qt. saucepan. Cook over medium heat, stirring constantly, until mixture comes to a boil. Boil 1 minute more. Add raspberries and cool thoroughly.

Chunky Lentil Soup*

Grilled Ham-and-Cheese Rolls*

Carrot Relish*

Chocolate Pound Cake*

After the final whistle, recap the results over mugs of steaming *Chunky Lentil Soup* while ham and cheese sandwiches heat over the coals. *Marinated Carrot Relish* was developed by an Ohio farm woman and will add a touch of color and flavor to this soup-and-sandwich lunch. It needs no cooking—just toss shredded carrots together with a homemade vinegar dressing and marinate several hours. The relish will keep for several days in the refrigerator and for several weeks in the freezer. If you like chocolate, you'll love *Chocolate Pound Cake*. It's a high-volume cake with a moist, tender crumb and rich cocoa flavor. It looks party-perfect sprinkled with confectioners' sugar.

Chunky Lentil Soup

1 lb. ground chuck
1 c. dried lentils, rinsed
1 c. diced, pared carrots
1 c. chopped celery
1 c. chopped cabbage
1 c. chopped onion
1 tsp. finely chopped green pepper
1 tsp. salt
½ tsp. pepper
1 bay leaf
2 beef bouillon cubes
1 (46-oz.) can tomato juice (5¾ c.)
4 c. water

IN ADVANCE:

Cook ground chuck in a 6-qt. Dutch oven over medium heat until well-browned. Drain fat from Dutch oven. Add remaining ingredients and cook over high heat until mixture comes to a boil. Reduce heat to low.

Simmer, uncovered, 1½ hours or until lentils are tender. Pour into bowl, cover and refrigerate; or pour into thermos jugs.

TO REHEAT:

Warm soup over medium heat in a 6-qt. Dutch oven 30 to 35 minutes or until hot and bubbly. Makes about 3 qt. or 12 servings.

Grilled Ham-and-Cheese Rolls

½ lb. fully cooked ham, chopped
½ lb. pasteurized process American cheese, shredded
½ c. chili sauce
¼ c. finely chopped onion
2 hard-cooked eggs, chopped
3 tblsp. chopped sweet pickles
3 tblsp. mayonnaise
12 frankfurter rolls

Combine all ingredients except frankfurter rolls in bowl; mix well.

Place each frankfurter roll on a 10″ length of heavy-duty foil and fill with an equal amount of ham mixture. Securely wrap each roll into a loose packet and refrigerate.

TO GRILL:

Cook sandwich packets 4″ from gray coals (medium heat). Grill 15 to 20 minutes or until cheese is melted. Makes 12 servings.

Carrot Relish

2 c. sugar
1 c. cider vinegar
2 tsp. salt
1 tsp. celery seed
7 c. shredded, pared carrots
1 c. chopped onion

IN ADVANCE:

Combine sugar, vinegar, salt and celery seed in large bowl. Mix well. Add carrots and onion. Toss lightly to mix well.

Cover and refrigerate several hours before serving; or, place in freezer container, cover and freeze.

TO SERVE:

Thaw at room temperature 3 hours. Makes 6 c.

Chocolate Pound Cake

3 c. sifted flour
⅓ c. baking cocoa
½ tsp. baking powder
½ tsp. salt
1 c. butter or regular margarine
½ c. shortening
3 c. sugar
5 eggs
1 tsp. vanilla
1¼ c. milk
sifted confectioners' sugar

IN ADVANCE:

Sift together flour, cocoa, baking powder and salt; set aside.

Cream together butter, shortening and sugar in mixing bowl until light and fluffy, using an electric mixer at medium speed. Add eggs one at a time, beating well after each addition. Blend in vanilla (total beating time: about 10 minutes).

Add dry ingredients alternately with milk to creamed mixture, beating well after each addition. Sprinkle greased 10″ fluted tube pan with cocoa. Pour batter into prepared pan.

Bake in 325° oven 1 hour 30 minutes or until cake tester inserted in center comes out clean. Cool in pan on rack 10 minutes.

Remove from pan; cool completely on rack. Sprinkle with sifted confectioners' sugar. Makes 12 servings.

Smoky Barbecued Chicken*

Patio Baked Beans*

Corn Meal-Bran Muffins*

Cranberry Nog*

As the leaves turn from green to glorious shades of orange and gold and the air becomes crisp, many appetites peak. A hearty casserole of Patio Baked Beans is guaranteed to cure a case of the super-hungries. Grace your table with autumn leaves and Smoky Barbecued Chicken—a year 'round favorite of one North Dakota farm wife. The tomato-based barbecue sauce is sparked with a healthy splash of Tabasco and sweetened slightly with maple syrup. Corn Meal-Bran Muffins have a surprisingly light texture, yet are deliciously filling. Wash them down with Cranberry Nog; a cousin to the classic egg nog, it's made with heavy cream and enriched with eggs.

Smoky Barbecued Chicken

⅔ c. ketchup
⅔ c. hickory-flavored barbecue sauce
½ c. maple-flavored syrup
⅓ c. chopped onion
½ tsp. Tabasco sauce
2 (2½- to 3-lb.) broiler-fryers, cut up

Combine all ingredients except chicken in glass bowl. Mix well.

Dip chicken pieces in sauce and arrange in 15½x10½x1″ jelly roll pan. Pour remaining sauce over chicken.

Bake in 350° oven 1 hour 15 minutes or until tender. Makes 8 servings.

Patio Baked Beans

5 strips bacon
½ c. chopped onion
⅓ c. brown sugar, packed
1 tblsp. vinegar
¼ c. water
1 tsp. dry mustard
1 tsp. instant coffee powder
2 (28-oz.) cans pork and beans in tomato sauce

Fry bacon in 10″ skillet over medium heat until almost crisp. Remove bacon with slotted spoon and drain on paper towels. Cut into 1″ pieces. Set aside.

Sauté onion in 2 tblsp. bacon drippings until tender (do not brown). Add brown sugar, vinegar, water, mustard, coffee powder, beans and bacon. Cook over medium heat until mixture comes to a boil.

Remove from heat. Turn into 2-qt. glass casserole.

Bake in 350° oven 1 hour or until hot and bubbly. Makes 8 servings.

Corn Meal-Bran Muffins

1¼ c. all-bran cereal
1¼ c. milk
¾ c. stirred whole-wheat flour
½ c. sifted flour (all-purpose)
⅓ c. yellow corn meal
½ c. dark brown sugar, packed
3 tsp. baking powder
½ tsp. salt
1 egg, slightly beaten
⅓ c. cooking oil

IN ADVANCE:

Combine cereal and milk in bowl. Let stand 5 minutes.

Meanwhile, stir together whole-wheat flour, all-purpose flour, corn meal, brown sugar, baking powder and salt in another bowl. Set aside.

Add egg and oil to cereal mixture; mix well. Add to dry ingredients, stirring just enough to moisten. Spoon into greased 3″ muffin-pan cups.

Bake in 400° oven 20 minutes or until done. Cool completely and wrap in foil (or serve immediately). Makes 12 muffins.

TO REHEAT:

Warm foil-wrapped muffins in 350° oven 10 to 12 minutes or until hot.

Cranberry Nog

6 eggs, separated
1 c. sugar
2 c. half-and-half
3 (6-oz.) cans frozen cranberry juice
   concentrate, thawed
2 c. water
3 c. heavy cream

IN ADVANCE:

Combine egg yolks and ½ c. of the sugar in large bowl. Beat until thick and lemon-colored, about 5 minutes, using an electric mixer at high speed.

Blend in half-and-half, cranberry juice concentrate, water and 1 c. of the heavy cream, using an electric mixer at low speed. Set aside.

Beat egg whites in another large bowl until frothy, using an electric mixer at high speed. Gradually beat in remaining ½ c. sugar. Continue beating until soft peaks form.

Whip remaining 2 c. heavy cream in large bowl until stiff peaks form. Fold whipped cream into egg white mixture. Then fold in yolk mixture. Refrigerate.

TO SERVE:

Stir nog thoroughly and pour into punch bowl or large pitcher. Makes about 1 gal. or 16 (8-oz.) servings.

Index

A

A Complete Meal on the Grill, 92
A Family Reunion, 54
A Meal in the Field, 128
A Moveable Feast, 50
Alfresco American-style, 14
All-American Cookout, 66
American Heritage Barbecue, 40
Amish Oatmeal Cookies, 33
Angel Food Squares, Toasted, 31
Anytime, Anyplace Picnic, 114
Appetizer(s)
    Barbecued Chicken Wings, 86
    Chicken Livers wrapped in Bacon, 64
    Chilled Cranberry Soup, 40
    Cucumber Dip, 74
    Deviled Party Eggs, 54
    Frank-and-Pineapple Kabobs, 92
    Mexican Montage, 36
    Miniature Quiches, 98
    Minted Grapefruit-Orange Sections, 12
    Stuffed Cherry Tomatoes, 108
    Stuffed Mushroom Kabobs, 10
Apple(s)
    Alfresco, 121
    Cider, Cranberry-, 113
    Crisp, Orange-Coconut-, 77
    Nectar, Tangerine-, 85
    -Walnut Mold, 117
Applesauce Cake, Old-fashioned, 113
Apricot Bars, 119
Autumn Table, 134
Avocado
    Guacamole Salad, 63
    Salad Dressing, 123

B

Back-to-School Barbecue, 110
Backyard Barbecue, 24
Bacon
    -Cheese Macaroni, 128
    Chicken Livers wrapped in, 64
    -Corn Muffins, Cheesy, 123
    Omelet, Potato-, 13
    -Onion Rolls, 61
    -Onion Sticks, 50
Baked
    Alaska, Party, 91
    Beans, Patio, 134
    Beans, Super, 126
    Potatoes with Cheddar Cheese, 73
Baking Powder Biscuits, Flaky, 93
Banana
    Boats, Grilled, 97
    Cake with Penuche Frosting, 105
    Split Pie, 19
Barbecue
    Sauce, Butter, 110
    Slaw, 23
    Tools, 6
Barbecued. *See also* Grilled
    Beef Buns, 112
    Chicken in a Bag, 104
    Chicken Wings, 86
    Corn, 73
Bars, Grill-baked Butterscotch, 93
Basic Pastry, 98
Basil Beans and Tomatoes, 79
Bean(s)
    Cassoulet, Two-Step, 106
    Patio Baked, 134
    Salad, Kidney, 116
    Super Baked, 126
    Sweet-and-Sour Baked, 103
    and Tomatoes, Basil, 79

Beef
  Buns, Barbecued, 112
  Ground
    'n' Egg Loaves, 128
    Grilled Hamburgers, 66
    Hobo Meat Loaves, 92
    Loaves, Butter-barbecued, 110
    Olive-stuffed Meatballs, 52
    Pioneer Drumsticks, 72
    Pizza Burgers, 20
    Stuffed Big Burger, 32
    Taco Salad, 88
  Roast
    Marinated Chuck, 96
    on a Spit, Rolled, 94
  Steak
    Kabobs, Marinated, 80
    London Broil, 28
    with Sauce New Orleans, 10
    Strips, Grilled, 37
    Teriyaki Flank, 42
  Tacos, Kansas-style, 62
  Texican Chili, 122
Beverages
  Cold
    Cranberry Nog, 135
    Fruit Cooler, 39
    Ice Cream Sodas, Choco-Nut, 21
    Iced Mocha Float, 57
    Lemon-Lime Freeze, 115
    Lemony Iced Tea, 77
    Lime Slush Punch, 87
    Limeade, 63
    Melonade Cooler, 61
    Orange-Cider Punch, 75
    Pina Colada Flip, 25
    Raspberry-Lemon Fizz, 59
    Sangria, 89
    Sparkling Citrus Punch, 55
    Strawberry-Pineapple Flip, 47
    Summer Sparkle Punch, 51
    Super Cyder Floats, 43
    Tangerine-Apple Nectar, 85
  Hot
    Cranberry-Apple Cider, 113
    Frothy Mocha Cocoa, 127
Big-Batch Chicken Barbecue, 54

Big Burger Bun, 32
Biscuits, Flaky Baking Powder, 93
Bisque, Curried Squash, 48
Block Party Barbecue, 70
Blue Cheese Dressing, 37
Blue Sky Supper, 116
Blueberry
  Cake, Easy Fresh, 63
  Cake Squares, 51
  Grunt, 85
Bologna-Pickle Spread, 16
Bran Muffins, Corn Meal-, 135
Bratwurst and Onions, 120
Bread(s)
  Buttery Blue Cheese Loaf, 29
  Garlic Bubble Loaf, 25
  Health Crackers, 75
  Herbed French, 109
  Quick
    Brown Sugar Tea, 15
    Cheesy Bacon-Corn Muffins, 123
    Cheesy Whole-wheat Loaf, 31
    Corn Meal-Bran Muffins, 135
    Flaky Baking Powder Biscuits, 93
    Johnnycake, 77
    Make-ahead Popovers, 83
    Parmesan Cheese Crescents, 35
    Zucchini Nut, 115
  Snappy Cheddar Loaf, 107
  Surprise Pizza Rolls, 87
  Swiss Rye Loaf, 47
  Yeast
    Bacon-Onion Rolls, 61
    Bacon-Onion Sticks, 50
    Big Burger Bun, 32
    Cottage Cheese Rolls, 57
    Frankfurter Buns, 120
    Honey-Nut Rolls, 13
    Rolls, Refrigerated, 69
    Whole-wheat Batter, 23
    Whole-wheat Buns, 16
    Whole-wheat Pita, 49
Broccoli-Egg Salad, 29
Brown Sugar Tea Bread, 15
Brownies
  Outdoor, 67
  Peanut Butter, 129

Bun(s)
  Barbecued Beef, 112
  Big Burger, 32
  Frankfurter, 120
  Whole-wheat, 16
Burger, Stuffed Big, 32
Butter Barbecue Sauce, 110
Butter-barbecued Beef Loaves, 110
Buttermilk Soup, Chilled, 83
Butternut Squash and Peas, 109
Butterscotch Bars, Grill-baked, 93
Buttery Blue Cheese Loaf, 29

C

Cake(s)
  Chocolate Pound, 133
  Easy Fresh Blueberry, 63
  Elegant Strawberry Torte, 35
  Kathy's Hot Water Chocolate, 127
  Lazy Daisy, 103
  Marble Squares à la Mode, 59
  Mexican Chocolate, 89
  Old-fashioned Applesauce, 113
  Peach Upside-down, 11
  with Penuche Frosting, Banana, 105
  Russian Torte, 95
  Squares, Blueberry, 51
Campers' Choice, 72
Cantonese-style Vegetables, 18
Carefree Chicken Barbecue, 46
Carrot(s)
  Pickled, 27
  Relish, 133
Cassoulet, Two-Step Bean, 106
Charcoal
  Cooking Know-How, 7
  Grills, 5
Checking the Coals, 7
Cheese
  Baked Potatoes with, 73
  Cheesy
    Bacon-Corn Muffins, 123
    Potato Casserole, 97
    Potato Strips, 11
    Whole-wheat Loaf, 31
  Cottage Cheese Rolls, 57
  Crescents, Parmesan, 35

Dressing, Blue, 37
Eggplant au Gratin, 52
Grilled Potatoes au Gratin, 27
Loaf, Buttery Blue, 29
Macaroni, Bacon-, 128
Pie, Pumpkin, 125
Ring, Pineapple-, 19
Rolls, Grilled Ham-and-, 132
Snappy Cheddar Loaf, 107
-stuffed Potatoes, 94
Swiss Rye Loaf, 47
Chef's Salad, Special, 119
Cherry Tomatoes, Stuffed, 108
Chicken
  in a Bag, Barbecued, 104
  Barbecue, Big-Batch, 54
  Barbecue, Herbed, 22
  in a Basket, 34
  Chowder, Parslied, 118
  Crispy Fried, 34
  Lemon-Rosemary Drumsticks, 130
  Livers wrapped in Bacon, 64
  Salad on Rye, Chunky, 38
  Smoky Barbecued, 134
  with Sweet Potatoes, 46
  Wings, Barbecued, 86
Chili Sauce, Peppery, 109
Chili, Texican, 122
Chilled
  Buttermilk Soup, 83
  Cranberry Soup, 40
  Peach Squares, 53
Chocolate
  Cake, Kathy's Hot Water, 127
  Cake, Mexican, 89
  Choco-Mint Ice Cream Sodas, 21
  Frosting, 89
  Frosting, Fluffy, 127
  Fudge Sauce, 59
  Hard-Hat Ice Cream Sundaes, 79
  Hot Fudge Sauce, 81
  Peanut Butter Brownies, 129
  Pound Cake, 133
Choco-Mint Ice Cream Sodas, 21
Chowder(s)
  Easy Salmon, 112
  Parslied Chicken, 118

Chuckwagon Special, 122
Chunky Chicken Salad on Rye, 38
Chunky Lentil Soup, 132
Cider, Cranberry-Apple, 113
Cider Punch, Orange-, 75
Cinnamon Pears, 111
City-style Cookout, 52
Cleanup, 8
Cocoa, Frothy Mocha, 127
Cocoa Mix, Homemade, 13
Coconut
    -Apple Crisp, Orange-, 77
    -Pecan Topping, 103
Coleslaw
    Pepper Cups, 67
    Tangy, 55
Community Cookout, 86
Compote, Fresh Fruit, 99
Confectioners' Sugar Icing, 107
Confetti Rice Salad, 34
Cookies
    Amish Oatmeal, 33
    Apricot Bars, 119
    English Shortbread, 115
    Family-style, 123
    Frosted Spice Squares, 107
    Grill-baked Butterscotch Bars, 93
    Jumbo Oatmeal-Peanut Butter, 17
    Marathon, 39
    Outdoor Brownies, 67
    Peanut Butter Brownies, 129
Corn
    Barbecued, 73
    Meal-Bran Muffins, 135
    Muffins, Cheesy Bacon-, 123
Cornish Hens à l'Orange, 18
Cottage Cheese Rolls, 57
Courtyard Cuisine, 62
Covered Kettle Cookers, 5
Crackers, Health, 75
Cranberry
    -Apple Cider, 113
    Nog, 135
    -Orange Salad, 125
    Soup, Chilled, 40
Creamy Potato Boats, 28

Crisp, Orange-Coconut-Apple, 77
Crisp, Strawberry-Rhubarb, 27
Crispy Fried Chicken, 34
Crowd, Enough for a, 1
    Chart, 2
Crust, Pretzel, 75
Cucumber(s)
    Dip, 74
    Frozen Cuke and Onion Relish, 39
    Mold, Dilly, 47
    in Sour Cream, 41
    -Yogurt Sauce, 49
Curried
    Sour Cream Dip with Fresh
        Vegetables, 99
    Squash Bisque, 48
    Stuffing, Roaster on a Spit with, 68

D
Danish Potato Salad, 20
Dessert(s)
    Blueberry Grunt, 85
    Cake(s)
        Chocolate Pound, 133
        Easy Fresh Blueberry, 63
        Elegant Strawberry Torte, 35
        Kathy's Hot Water Chocolate, 127
        Lazy Daisy, 103
        Marble Squares à la Mode, 59
        Mexican Chocolate, 89
        Old-fashioned Applesauce, 113
        Peach Upside-down, 11
        with Penuche Frosting, Banana, 105
        Russian Torte, 95
        Squares, Blueberry, 51
        Toasted Angel Food Squares, 31
    Chilled Buttermilk Soup, 83
    Chilled Peach Squares, 53
    Cookies
        Amish Oatmeal, 33
        Apricot Bars, 119
        English Shortbread, 115
        Family-style, 123
        Frosted Spice Squares, 107
        Grill-baked Butterscotch Bars, 93
        Jumbo Oatmeal-Peanut Butter, 17
        Marathon, 39

Cookies (continued)
  Outdoor Brownies, 67
  Peanut Butter Brownies, 129
Frosty Strawberry Torte, 117
Fruit
  Apples Alfresco, 121
  Cinnamon Pears, 111
  Compote, Fresh, 99
  Grilled Banana Boats, 97
  Grilled Whole Pineapple, 69
  Pears in Mint Sauce, 15
Ice Cream
  Banana Split Pie, 19
  'n' Pretzel Pie, 75
  Sodas, Choco-Mint, 21
  Sundaes
    Hard-Hat, 79
    Peach, 49
    Praline, 33
    Vanilla-Walnut, 37
  Vanilla, 80
Ice Creamwiches, 41
Orange-Coconut-Apple Crisp, 77
Orange Sherbet Molds
  with Strawberries, 71
Party Baked Alaska, 91
Pie(s)
  Banana Split, 19
  Ice Cream 'n' Pretzel, 75
  Pumpkin Cheese, 125
Raspberry-Vanilla Cloud, 131
Sauce(s)
  Fudge, 59
    Hot, 81
  Maraschino Cherry, 99
  Mint, 15
  Peanut Butter, 81
  Raspberry, 131
S'mores, 73
Strawberry-Rhubarb Crisp, 27
Deviled Party Eggs, 54
Dilly Cucumber Mold, 47
Dinner for a Dozen, 108
Dip(s)
  with Fresh Vegetables, Sour Cream, 99
  Peppery Peanut, 86
Drumsticks, Lemon-Rosemary, 130

E

Easy Fresh Blueberry Cake, 63
Easy Salmon Chowder, 112
Easy Spinach Souffle, 43
Egg(s)
  Deviled Party, 54
  Eggciting Potato Salad, 66
  Potato-Bacon Omelet, 13
  Salad(s)
    Broccoli-, 29
    Supreme, Macaroni-, 71
Eggciting Potato Salad, 66
Eggplant au Gratin, 52
Electric Grills, 6
Elegant Strawberry Torte, 35
English Shortbread, 115
Enough for a Crowd, 1
  Chart, 2
Equipping the Outdoor Kitchen, 5

F

Family-style Cookies, 123
Father's Day Favorites, 58
Filling, Herb, 108
Flaky Baking Powder Biscuits, 93
Fluffy Chocolate Frosting, 127
Fourth of July Picnic, 68
Frankfurter(s)
  Buns, 120
  -and-Pineapple Kabobs, 92
  Potato Salad, Hot, 50
  Stuffed, 102
Fresh Fruit Compote, 99
Fresh Fruit Salad, 57
Fresh Fruit Slush, 17
Fried Chicken, Crispy, 34
Frosted Spice Squares, 107
Frosting(s). *See also* Icings
  Chocolate, 89
  Fluffy Chocolate, 127
  Penuche, 105
Frosty Strawberry Torte, 117
Frothy Mocha Cocoa, 127
Frozen Cuke and Onion Relish, 39

Fruit
   Apples Alfresco, 121
   Basket, Watermelon, 90
   Cinnamon Pears, 111
   Compote, Fresh, 99
   Cooler, 39
   Fruity Rice Salad, 79
   Grilled Banana Boats, 97
   Grilled Whole Pineapple, 69
   Guacamole Salad, 63
   Kabobs, 21
   -Nut Mix, 102
   Pears in Mint Sauce, 15
   Salad, Fresh, 57
   Salad, Macaroni-, 14
   Slush, Fresh, 17
Fruity Rice Salad, 79
Fudge Sauce, 59
   Hot, 81

G

Garden Salad, 105
Garlic Bubble Loaf, 25
Gas Grills, 6
Gazpacho, Souper, 88
Gelatin Molds
   Apple-Walnut, 117
   Cranberry-Orange Salad, 125
   Dilly Cucumber, 47
   Pineapple-Cheese Ring, 19
   Ring, Red, White and Blue, 68
German Potato Salad, 121
Ginger-glazed Spareribs, 70
Golden Rice Pilaf, 43
Gourmet at the Grill, 130
Graduation Day Buffet, 32
Grapefruit-Orange Sections, Minted, 12
Green Beans
   with Almonds, 25
   Herbed, 111
Grill(s)
   Covered Kettle Cookers, 5
   Gas and Electric, 6
   Open Braziers, 5
   Rectangular, 6

Grill-baked Butterscotch Bars, 93
Grilled
   Beef
      Ground
         Hamburgers, 66
         Hobo Meat Loaves, 92
         Loaves, Butter-barbecued, 110
         Olive-stuffed Meatballs, 52
         Pioneer Drumsticks, 72
         Pizza Burgers, 20
         Stuffed Big Burger, 32
      Roast
         Marinated Chuck, 96
         on a Spit, Rolled, 94
      Steak
         Kabobs, Marinated, 80
         London Broil, 28
         with Sauce New Orleans, 10
         Strips, 37
         Teriyaki Flank, 42
   Bread(s)
      Buttery Blue Cheese Loaf, 29
      Herbed French, 109
      Snappy Cheddar Loaf, 107
      Swiss Rye Loaf, 47
   Desserts
      Apples Alfresco, 121
      Banana Boats, 97
      Cinnamon Pears, 111
      Grill-baked Butterscotch Bars, 93
      Outdoor Brownies, 67
      S'mores, 73
      Toasted Angel Food Squares, 31
   Fruit
      Kabobs, 21
      Whole Pineapple, 69
   Lamb
      Breast, Stuffed, 26
      Kabobs, 84
      Leg of Lamb, 109
      Mixed Grill, 58
   Pork
      Chop(s)
         Honey-barbecued, 56
         with Orange-Apple Stuffing, 24
         and Pineapple on a Spit, 82
         Suppers, 30

Grilled
  Pork (continued)
    Cubes
      Kabobs, Marinated, 48
      with Peppery Peanut Dip, 86
    Ham
      Barbecue Sandwiches, 126
      -and-Cheese Rolls, 132
    Roast, Marinated, 116
    Spareribs
      Ginger-glazed, 70
      Louise's Luau, 65
      Saucy, 78
  Poultry
    Chicken
      Barbecue, Big-Batch, 54
      Barbecue, Herbed, 22
      Lemon-Rosemary Drumsticks, 130
      Livers wrapped in Bacon, 64
      Roaster on a Spit with Curried
        Stuffing, 68
      with Sweet Potatoes, 46
      Wings, Barbecued, 86
    Cornish Hens à l'Orange, 18
    Turkey
      Herbed Split, 124
      on a Spit, Sausage-stuffed, 41
  Sausage
    Bratwurst and Onions, 120
    Frank-and-Pineapple Kabobs, 92
    Kabobs, Italian, 60
    Kielbasa and Mushroom Suppers, 76
    Stuffed Franks, 102
  Vegetable(s)
    Baked Potatoes with Cheddar
      Cheese, 73
    Barbecued Corn, 73
    Basil Beans and Tomatoes, 79
    Cantonese-style, 18
    Cheesy Potato Casserole, 97
    Cheesy Potato Strips, 11
    Creamy Potato Boats, 29
    Eggplant au Gratin, 52
    Green Beans with Almonds, 25
    Grill-baked Sweet Potatoes, 124
    Herbed Cherry Tomatoes, 97
    Herbed Corn on the Grill, 71

Grilled
  Vegetables (continued)
    Herbed Green Beans, 111
    Kabobs, Mixed, 65
    Peas and Mushrooms, 130
    Potatoes au Gratin, 27
    Ratatouille, 58
    Stuffed Mushroom Kabobs, 10
    -stuffed Zucchini, 83
Grunt, Blueberry, 85
Guacamole Salad, 63

H

Ham
  Barbecue Sandwiches, 126
  -and-Cheese Rolls, Grilled, 132
Happy Birthday Barbecue, 80
Hard-Hat Ice Cream Sundaes, 79
Hawaiian Luau, 64
Health Crackers, 75
Heat Deflector, 6
Herb Filling, 108
Herbed
  Cherry Tomatoes, 97
  Chicken Barbecue, 22
  Corn on the Grill, 71
  French Bread, 109
  Green Beans, 111
  Split Turkey, 124
Hibachis, 5
Hobo Meat Loaves, 92
Homemade Cocoa Mix, 13
Honey
  -barbecued Pork Chops, 56
  Dressing, 117
  -Nut Rolls, 13
Hot Frank Potato Salad, 50
Hot Fudge Sauce, 81
How to Estimate Food for a Crowd, 1

I

Ice Cream
  Banana Split Pie, 19

Ice Cream (continued)
  Beverages
    Iced Mocha Float, 57
    Sodas, Choco-Mint, 21
    Super Cyder Floats, 43
  Ice Creamwiches, 41
  'n' Pretzel Pie, 75
  Sauce(s)
    Fudge, 59
    Hot Fudge, 81
    Peanut Butter, 81
  Sundaes
    Hard-Hat, 79
    Peach, 49
    Praline, 33
    Vanilla-Walnut, 37
  Vanilla, 80
Ice Creamwiches, 41
Iced Mocha Float, 57
Icing(s)
  Confectioners' Sugar, 107
  Orange, 119
Impromptu Picnic, 38
In Advance, 1
Italian Sausage Kabobs, 60

J

Johnnycake, 77
Jumbo Oatmeal-Peanut Butter
  Cookies, 17

K

Kabobs
  Frank-and-Pineapple, 92
  Fruit, 21
  Italian Sausage, 60
  Lamb, 84
  Marinated Beef, 80
  Marinated Pork, 48
  Mixed Vegetable, 65
  Stuffed Mushroom, 10
Kansas-style Beef Tacos, 62
Kathy's Hot Water Chocolate Cake, 127

Kidney Bean Salad, 116
Kielbasa and Mushroom Suppers, 76

L

Labor Day Recess, 106
Lamb
  Breast, Stuffed, 26
  Kabobs, 84
  Leg of, 109
  Mixed Grill, 58
Landlubber's Lunch, 112
Layered Salmon Salad, 74
Lazy Daisy Cake, 103
Lazy Day Barbecue, 96
Leg of Lamb, 109
Lemon
  Fizz, Raspberry-, 59
  -Lime Freeze, 115
  -Rosemary Drumsticks, 130
Lemony Iced Tea, 77
Lentil
  Salad, 111
  Soup, Chunky, 132
Let It Rain!, 8
Lime
  Freeze, Lemon-, 115
  Slush Punch, 87
Limeade, 63
Little League Banquet, 90
London Broil, 28
Louise's Luau Spareribs, 65
Low-Cal
  Cookout, 22
  Scalloped Potatoes, 23

M

Macaroni
  Bacon-Cheese, 128
  -Egg Salad Supreme, 71
  -Fruit Salad, 14
Main-Dish Potato Salad, 114
Make-ahead Popovers, 83
Maraschino Cherry Sauce, 99
Marathon Cookies, 39
Marble Squares à la Mode, 59

Marinated
    Beef Kabobs, 80
    Chuck Roast, 96
    Pork Kabobs, 48
    Pork Roast, 116
    Vegetables, 95
May Day Feast, 18
Meat Loaves
    Beef 'n' Egg, 128
    Butter-barbecued Beef, 110
    Hobo, 92
Melonade Cooler, 61
Meringue, 91
Mexican
    Chocolate Cake, 89
    Montage, 36
    Salad Bowl, 122
    -style Supper, 36
Midsummer Night's Supper, 74
Miniature Quiches, 98
Mint
    Ice Cream Sodas, Choco-, 21
    Sauce, Pears in, 15
Minted Grapefruit-Orange Sections, 12
Mix, Homemade Cocoa, 13
Mixed Grill, 58
Mixed Vegetable Kabobs, 65
Mocha Float, Iced, 57
Mock Russian Dressing, 107
Mother's Day Barbecue, 28
Muffins
    Cheesy Bacon-Corn, 123
    Corn Meal-Bran, 135
Mushroom(s)
    Kabobs, Stuffed, 10
    Peas and, 130
    Suppers, Kielbasa and, 76

N

Nut(s)
    Bread, Zucchini, 115
    Coconut-Pecan Topping, 103
    Mix, Fruit-, 102
    Rolls, Honey-, 13
    Russian Torte, 95

Nut(s) (continued)
    Vanilla-Walnut Sundaes, 37

O

Oatmeal
    Cookies, Amish, 33
    -Peanut Butter Cookies, Jumbo, 17
Octoberfest, 120
Oil and Vinegar Dressing, 118
Old-fashioned Applesauce Cake, 113
Olive-stuffed Meatballs, 52
Omelet, Potato-Bacon, 13
Onion
    Rolls, Bacon-, 60
    Salad, Tomato-, 53
    Sticks, Bacon-, 50
Open Braziers, 5
Orange
    -Cider Punch, 75
    -Coconut-Apple Crisp, 77
    Icing, 119
    Salad, Cranberry-, 125
    Sections, Minted Grapefruit-, 12
    Sherbet Molds with Strawberries, 71
Outdoor Brownies, 67
Outdoor Kitchen Cookery, 78
Oven-style Rib Barbecue, 14
Overnight Tossed Green Salad, 60

P

Packing the Picnic Basket, 1
    Keeping foods colds, 3
    Keeping foods hot, 3
    Keeping foods safe, 3
Parade Party, 42
Parmesan Cheese Crescents, 35
Parslied Chicken Chowder, 118
Party Baked Alaska, 91
Pastry, Basic, 98
Patio Baked Beans, 134
Peach
    Ice Cream Sundaes, 49
    Squares, Chilled, 53
    Upside-down Cake, 11

Peanut Butter
    Brownies, 129
    Cookies, Jumbo Oatmeal-, 17
    Glaze, 129
    Pork with Peppery Peanut Dip, 86
    Sauce, 81
Pears
    Cinnamon, 111
    in Mint Sauce, 15
Peas
    Butternut Squash and, 109
    and Mushrooms, 130
Pecan Topping, Coconut-, 103
Penuche Frosting, 105
Peppery Chili Sauce, 109
Peppery Peanut Dip, 86
Pick-Me-Up Picnic, 16
Pick-Up-and-Go Picnic, 76
Pickled Carrots, 27
Picnic in a Bag, 104
Pie(s)
    Banana Split, 19
    Ice Cream 'n' P   tzel, 75
    Pumpkin Cheese, 125
Pilaf, Golden Rice, 43
Pilgrims' Picnic, 124
Pina Colada Flip, 25
Pineapple
    -Cheese Ring, 19
    Flip, Strawberry-, 47
    Grilled Whole, 69
    Kabobs, Frank-and-, 92
    on a Spit, Pork and, 82
Pioneer Drumsticks, 72
Pita, Whole-wheat, 49
Pizza
    Burger Barbecue, 20
    Burgers, 20
    Rolls, Surprise, 87
Popovers, Make-ahead, 83
Pork
    Chops
        Honey-barbecued, 56
        with Orange-Apple Stuffing, 24
        and Pineapple on a Spit, 82
        Suppers, 30

Pork (continued)
    Cubes
        Kabobs, Marinated, 48
        with Peppery Peanut Dip, 86
        Two-Step Bean Cassoulet, 106
    Ham
        Barbecue Sandwiches, 126
        -and-Cheese Rolls, Grilled, 132
    Roast, Marinated, 116
    Sausage
        Bratwurst and Onions, 120
        Kabobs, Italian, 60
        Kielbasa and Mushroom Suppers, 76
        Mixed Grill, 58
        Stuffed Mushroom Kabobs, 10
    Spareribs
        Barbecue, Oven-style, 14
        Ginger-glazed, 70
        Louise's Luau, 65
        Saucy Ribs, 78
Post-Game Warm-Up, 132
Potato(es)
    -Bacon Omelet, 13
    Boats, Creamy, 28
    Casserole, Cheesy, 97
    with Cheddar Cheese, Baked, 73
    Cheese-stuffed, 94
    au Gratin, Grilled, 27
    Low-Cal Scalloped, 23
    Salad(s)
        Danish, 20
        German, 121
        Hot Frank, 50
        Main-Dish, 114
        Sour Cream, 90
    Strips, Cheesy, 11
Potlatch Picnic, 126
Poultry
    Chicken
        in a Bag, Barbecued, 104
        Barbecue, Big-Batch, 54
        Barbecue, Herbed, 22
        Crispy Fried, 34
        Lemon-Rosemary Drumsticks, 130
        Livers wrapped in Bacon, 64
        Roaster on a Spit with Curried
            Stuffing, 68

Poultry
   Chicken (continued)
      Salad on Rye, Chunky, 38
      Smoky Barbecued, 134
      with Sweet Potatoes, 46
      Wings, Barbecued, 86
   Cornish Hens à l'Orange, 18
   Turkey
      Herbed Split, 124
      on a Spit, Sausage-stuffed, 41
Praline Ice Cream Sundaes, 33
Prelude or Finale, 98
Pretzel Crust, 75
Pride of Iowa Barbecue, 56
Pumpkin Cheese Pie, 125
Punch(es)
   Cranberry Nog, 135
   Fruit Cooler, 39
   Lime Slush, 87
   Limeade, 63
   Orange-Cider, 75
   Pina Colada Flip, 25
   Sangria, 89
   Sparkling Citrus, 55
   Summer Sparkle, 51

Q

Quantity Cooking Chart, 2
Quiches, Miniature, 98
Quick Bread(s). *See* Bread(s)

R

Raspberry
   -Lemon Fizz, 59
   Sauce, 131
   -Vanilla Cloud, 131
Ratatouille, 58
Readying the Coals for Cooking, 7
Rectangular Grills, 6
Red, White and Blue Gelatin Ring, 68
Refrigerated Yeast Rolls, 69
Relish(es)
   Carrot, 133
   Frozen Cuke and Onion, 39
   Pickled Carrots, 27

Rhubarb Crisp, Strawberry-, 27
Rice
   Pilaf, Golden, 43
   Salad, Confetti, 34
   Salad, Fruity, 79
Roaster on a Spit with Curried
   Stuffing, 68
Rolled Roast on a Spit, 94
Rolls
   Bacon-Onion, 61
   Cottage Cheese, 57
   Honey-Nut, 13
   Refrigerated Yeast, 69
Russian Dressing, Mock, 107
Russian Torte, 95

S

Salad(s)
   Fruit
      Fresh, 57
      Fruity Rice Salad, 79
      Slush, Fresh, 17
      Watermelon Fruit Basket, 90
   Gelatin
      Apple-Walnut Mold, 117
      Cranberry-Orange, 125
      Dilly Cucumber Mold, 47
      Red, White and Blue Gelatin Ring, 68
   Macaroni
      -Egg Salad Supreme, 71
      -Fruit, 14
   Main-Dish
      Eggciting Potato, 66
      Layered Salmon, 74
      Potato Salad, 114
      on Rye, Chunky Chicken, 38
      Taco, 88
   Potato
      Danish, 20
      Eggciting, 66
      German, 121
      Hot Frank, 50
      Main-Dish, 114
      Sour Cream, 90

Salad(s) (continued)
  Vegetable
    Barbecue Slaw, 23
    Broccoli-Egg, 29
    Bowl, Mexican, 122
    Coleslaw Pepper Cups, 67
    Confetti Rice, 34
    Cucumbers in Sour Cream, 41
    Frozen Cuke and Onion Relish, 39
    Garden, 105
    Guacamole, 62
    with Hot Bacon Dressing,
      Spinach, 84
    Kidney Bean, 116
    Lentil, 111
    Marinated Vegetables, 95
    Overnight Tossed Green, 60
    Six-Vegetable, 128
    Special Chef's, 119
    Sweet Potato, 131
    Tangy Coleslaw, 55
    Tomato Cups, 113
    Tomato-Onion, 53
    Wilted Leaf Lettuce, 31
Salad Dressing(s)
  Avocado, 123
  Blue Cheese, 37
  Honey, 117
  Mock Russian, 107
  Oil and Vinegar, 118
  Vinaigrette, 105
  Zesty Tomato, 65
Salmon Chowder, Easy, 112
Salmon Salad, Layered, 74
Sandwiches
  Bratwurst and Onions, 120
  Chunky Chicken Salad on Rye, 38
  Grilled Ham-and-Cheese Rolls, 132
  Ham Barbecue, 126
  Pizza Burgers, 20
Sangria, 89
Sauce(s)
  Butter Barbecue, 110
  Cucumber-Yogurt, 49
  Fudge, 59
    Hot, 81
  Maraschino Cherry, 99

Sauce(s) (continued)
  Mint, 15
  Peanut Butter, 81
  Peppery Chili, 109
  Raspberry, 131
  Sweet-Sour, 128
Saucy Ribs, 78
Sausage
  Bratwurst and Onions, 120
  Frank-and-Pineapple Kabobs, 92
  Kabobs, Italian, 60
  Kielbasa and Mushroom Suppers, 76
  Stuffed Franks, 102
  -stuffed Turkey on a Spit, 41
Scalloped Potatoes, Low-Cal, 23
Shortbread, English, 115
Six-Vegetable Salad, 128
Smoky Barbecued Chicken, 134
S'mores, 73
Snappy Cheddar Loaf, 107
Sombrero Supper, 88
Soufflé, Easy Spinach, 43
Soup(s)
  Chilled Buttermilk, 83
  Chilled Cranberry, 40
  Chunky Lentil, 132
  Curried Squash Bisque, 48
  Easy Salmon Chowder, 112
  Parslied Chicken Chowder, 118
  'n' Sandwich Supper, 48
  Souper Gazpacho, 88
Sour Cream Potato Salad, 90
Spareribs
  Ginger-glazed, 70
  Louise's Luau, 65
  Saucy Ribs, 78
Sparkling Citrus Punch, 55
Special Chef's Salad, 119
Spinach
  Salad with Hot Bacon Dressing, 84
  Souffle, Easy, 43
"Spring Forward" Brunch, 12
Springtime Jubilee, 26
Square Dance Supper, 94
Squash
  Bisque, Curried, 48
  and Peas, Butternut, 109

Starting the fire, 7
Steak. *See also* Beef
Steak and Potatoes to Go, 10
Stop-and-Go Supper, 82
Strawberry(ies)
    Orange Sherbet Molds with, 71
    -Pineapple Flip, 47
    -Rhubarb Crisp, 27
    Torte, Elegant, 35
    Torte, Frosty, 117
Stuffed
    Big Burger, 32
    Cherry Tomatoes, 108
    Franks, 102
    Lamb Breast, 26
    Mushroom Kabobs, 10
Summer Sparkle Punch, 51
Summertime Sandwichery, 84
Super
    Baked Beans, 126
    Cyder Floats, 43
Supper on a Saber, 60
Surprise Pizza Rolls, 87
Surprise Supper, 30
Sweet Potato(es)
    Chicken with, 46
    Grill-baked, 124
    Salad, 131
Sweet-and-Sour Baked Beans, 103
Sweet-Sour Sauce, 128
Swiss Rye Loaf, 47

T

Taco Salad, 88
Tacos, Kansas-style, 62
Tailgate Picnic, 118
Tangerine-Apple Nectar, 85
Tangy Coleslaw, 55
Tea, Lemony Iced, 77
Ten Tips for Charcoal Grilling, 8
Teriyaki Flank Steak, 42
Texican Chili, 122
Tips for Carefree Picnicking, 5
Tips on Packing Foods, 4
To Grill, 1

Toasted Angel Food Squares, 31
Tomato(es)
    Basil Beans and, 79
    Cups, 113
    Dressing, Zesty, 65
    Herbed Cherry, 97
    -Onion Salad, 53
Topping, Coconut-Pecan, 103
Torte(s)
    Elegant Strawberry, 35
    Frosty Strawberry, 117
    Russian, 95
Trail Blazer's Barbecue, 102
Turkey
    Herbed Split, 124
    on a Spit, Sausage-stuffed, 41
Two-Step Bean Cassoulet, 106

U

Using These Recipes, 1
Using Your Grill as an Oven, 6

V

Vanilla
    Cloud, Raspberry-, 131
    Ice Cream, 80
    -Walnut Sundaes, 37
Vegetable(s)
    Bean(s)
        Cassoulet, Two-Step, 106
        Patio Baked, 134
        Super Baked, 126
        Sweet-and-Sour Baked, 103
    Broccoli-Egg Salad, 29
    Butternut Squash and Peas, 109
    Cabbage
        Coleslaw Pepper Cups, 67
        Tangy Coleslaw, 55
    Cantonese-style, 18
    Carrot(s)
        Pickled, 27
        Relish, 133
    Cherry Tomatoes
        Herbed, 97
        Stuffed, 108

Vegetable(s) (continued)
  Corn
    Barbecued, 73
    on the Grill, Herbed, 71
  Cucumber(s)
    Dip, 74
    Frozen Cuke and Onion Relish, 39
    Mold, Dilly, 47
    in Sour Cream, 41
    -Yogurt Sauce, 49
  Curried Sour Cream Dip with Fresh, 99
  Eggplant au Gratin, 52
  Green Beans
    with Almonds, 25
    Herbed, 111
    and Tomatoes, Basil, 79
  Guacamole Salad, 63
  Kabobs, Mixed, 65
  Kidney Bean Salad, 116
  Lentil
    Salad, 111
    Soup, Chunky, 132
  Lettuce
    Garden Salad, 105
    Mexican Salad Bowl, 122
    Wilted Leaf, 31
  Marinated, 95
  Mushroom Kabobs, Stuffed, 10
  Peas and Mushrooms, 130
  Potato(es)
    -Bacon Omelet, 13
    Boats, Creamy, 28
    Casserole, Cheesy, 97
    with Cheddar Cheese, Baked, 73
    au Gratin, Grilled, 27
    Low-Cal Scalloped, 23
    Salad(s)
      Danish, 20
      Eggciting, 66
      German, 121
      Main-Dish, 114
      Sour Cream, 90
    Strips, Cheesy, 11
  Ratatouille, 58
  Salad, Six-, 128

Vegetable(s) continued
  Spinach
    Salad with Hot Bacon Dressing, 84
    Soufflé, Easy, 43
  Squash Bisque, Curried, 48
  Sweet Potato(es)
    Chicken with, 46
    Grill-baked, 124
    Salad, 131
  Tomato(es)
    Basil Beans and, 79
    Cups, 113
    -Onion Salad, 53
  Zucchini
    Nut Bread, 115
    -stuffed, 83
Vinaigrette Dressing, 105

W

Walnut
  Mold, Apple-, 117
  Sundaes, Vanilla-, 37
Watermelon Fruit Basket, 90
Whole-wheat
  Batter Bread, 23
  Buns, 16
  Pita, 49
Wilted Leaf Lettuce, 31

Y

Yeast Breads. *See* Bread(s)
Yogurt Sauce, Cucumber-, 49

Z

Zesty Tomato Dressing, 65
Zucchini
  Nut Bread, 115
  Vegetable-stuffed, 83